Get Out of Debt Hell

Jen Pattison

Get Out of Debt Hell

I did it, and so can you

Jen Pattison

Cover design by Ryan Ashcroft
www.loveyourcovers.com

Formatting by Jo Harrison
www.ebook-formatting.co.uk

Copyright © Jen Pattison 2016
All rights reserved. No part of this publication may be reproduced, distributed, or transmitted in any form or by any means, including photocopying, recording, or other electronic or mechanical methods, without the prior written permission of the author, except in the case of brief quotations embodied in critical reviews and certain other non-commercial uses permitted by copyright law.

About the author

Jen Pattison is the pen name of a debt survivor. She would have preferred to write under her own name in order to reduce the stigma of debt hell, but some people close to her objected as they would be identified and she decided to respect their wishes. She lives with her husband of many years and they are presently taking some time out by house sitting after many stressful years of working in the public sector. She is using this time to take a breather, enjoy some hobbies, retrain for a new career, to reflect on the past and write.

Follow me on:

Facebook
https://www.facebook.com/getout ofdebthell/

Twitter
https://twitter.com/@JPattisonGOODH

Blog
jenpattison.wordpress.com

Disclaimer

This book is designed to provide information on debt problems only. This information is provided and sold with the knowledge that the author does not offer any legal or other professional advice. In case of a need for any such expertise consult with an appropriate professional. This book does not contain all information available on the subject and has not been created to be specific to any individual's situations or needs. Every effort has been made to make this book as accurate as possible, however this book contains information that may change and is intended only to educate and entertain. The author shall have no liability to any person or entity regarding any loss or damage incurred, or alleged to have incurred, directly or indirectly by the information contained in this book. The references and links to websites, books and films are provided for informational purposes only and do not constitute endorsement of any products or services. The information contained within this book is strictly for educational purposes and if you intend to apply ideas contained within this book you are taking full responsibility for your actions. You hereby agree to be bound by this disclaimer or you may return the book within the guaranteed time period for a full refund.

Contents

Introduction 1
My story - how I got into a mess of debt 8
The IVA – the end of a lifestyle of debt 17
The state of Britain today - and how it used to be 23
A culture that lures you to spend 36
Revise your spending 59
Planning your finances - and why many people don't 70
How to turn around your finances 75
Money-saving tips 88
Epilogue 104
Useful organisations 109
Recommended reading and viewing 112

To my husband and to Chris, two of my dearest friends; thanks for everything.

Introduction

The first step towards getting somewhere is to decide that you are not going to stay where you are.

- J.P Morgan

How could I have been so stupid?

That is what I ask myself when I look back at how I got into so much debt. The depth of the sheer stupidity became even more apparent to me as I wrote the story of the years in which I entered the workplace and started to spend, and how it left me with so little to show for all the money I had spent over the years. In many ways I am not a stupid person; apart from dealing with money I was a sensible, pragmatic and level-headed person throughout my debt-ridden years. This is an account of how I came to understand the influences that led me to get into so much debt, to overcome that and lead a debt-free life. I hope that it will help you too.

The burden of personal debt in Britain, and in many other countries, is the cause of deep misery and stress to thousands of people. Its pressures can cause or exacerbate mental illness and it leads some to suicide. Debt problems cause a great strain on relationships and can tear families apart. Many struggle alone with their debt problems as it is still considered a shameful subject and many keep the details of their crippling finances to themselves, whereas the reality is that they will probably have friends, family and colleagues who are also silently struggling with debt problems. Whether you have come to this book at the point where you have debts that are currently manageable but cause you a great deal of worry or you have reached the point where you are facing catastrophe imminently, the situation can be turned around – but you need to admit that you have a debt problem, and to be determined to do something about it. If you have reached the stage where you have no option but to use credit for your food shopping and other essential purchases, your problem is becoming serious.

There are many books available to guide you through the process of budgeting, rethinking your spending and reducing your debt but many do not place the problem of debt in a wider cultural context in any depth, or address the popular culture of spending in a significant way. Many books on getting out of debt are written by American authors and whilst the general principles are universal some of the advice is not relevant to Britain; for example a reference without clarification to 'your money in a 401(K)', that is only meaningful to Americans (it's a pension fund). That said, apart from the resources that I set out that are specific to Britain, the general principles of this book and my observations about society and culture are probably relevant to readers in other countries too.

I set out my story in this book against the backdrop of the culture that I grew up in; I was largely ignorant of its effect at the time on my behaviour and I didn't realise the degree to which overspending was compensating for my low self-esteem. It took many years before I realised fully the effect that popular culture had on me. I am not pointing the finger elsewhere for the mess that I found myself in however, I'm not claiming that "society and culture made me do it"; on the contrary, I am fully responsible for all the choices that I made. Placing the entirety of the blame elsewhere is victim mentality and casting yourself as a victim is a debilitating state of mind. Each of us has our unique character and we react to the effects of society and culture in different ways.

Hindsight is a wonderful thing though and I can't turn back the clock, but had I been more questioning and critical of the cultural forces around me as I grew up, maybe I would have made better choices about my finances. As I explored those cultural forces I came to understand that they are insidiously subtle and persuasive. In many ways I am a sensible and responsible person, but I never seemed to apply common sense to my spending until it came to the point where I was forced to do so. I hope that by explaining the cautionary tale of where I feel that I went wrong and the harmful influences that swayed me, I can help to guide you to change your thinking in a radical way by understanding and questioning the societal forces around you and to take control of your spending responsibly. I will start by looking at aspects of contemporary life in Britain that are leading to a general sense of insecurity in many people before telling my story of overspending and financial foolhardiness. I will examine how advertising, celebrity culture and the triumph of emotion over reason conspire subtly to induce you to spend, and the remainder of this book will explore solutions to help you to escape from the misery of debt and explore ways in which you can save money.

You may ask why the current state of Britain, advertising and celebrity culture are relevant to your debt problem, but no-one lives in a vacuum and I would argue that not many people think critically and deeply about the way the society around us influences how we think and feel. Many people unquestioningly take for granted what they see around them and it is only when you cast a critical eye on those influences that many illusions start to shatter. The Office for Budget Responsibility has announced that the total debt of Britons is expected to be £58 billion more than they earn in 2016 and that Britain's debt binge appears to have no end in sight[1], so it is clearly a problem that needs to be addressed if Britons are borrowing more than they earn. It is not a problem that will ever go away if the underlying causes are not examined and addressed.

I am not a financial wizard, nor am I a psychologist or counsellor. I am your ordinary person in the street who has come to look critically at how the ever-increasing burden of debt has come to plague our country today. This is my narrative of where I went wrong and what I see as wrong in the society around me. I have learned to question what I see in the world, to make connections and to come to conclusions. It is this process of thinking logically and critically of the society around us and how it influences us into making bad decisions that is essential if we are to come to a full understanding of how we come to make choices about our spending that are harmful to us. Once armed with that knowledge, it becomes much

---

[1] www.telegraph.co.uk/business/2016/03/17/household-debt-binge-has-no-end-in-sight-says-obr/

easier to turn away from it and to make wiser spending choices. To come to an understanding of how advertising, consumer culture, celebrity obsession, individualism and peer pressure shape our attitudes is not an excuse to justify your excessive spending – far from it! I hope that by outlining these subtle and insidious influences you will feel as angry as I was at not understanding them fully and being duped by them, and to follow me in rejecting them. You may not agree with everything that I say but I hope that you find it thought-provoking.

I'm sure that there are some people who will read this and think, "It's your own stupid fault for being so irresponsible". I have seen some similar comments on advice forums where people seek help in getting out of debt and some replies are along these lines. It is true, but it is neither helpful nor compassionate and I would say that it is intimidatory towards those who desperately need help and could deter them from seeking it. Congratulate yourself by all means if you have spent your entire life with a healthy and prudent attitude to money and have built up your assets to see you comfortably through life, but not everybody is the same as you. As the saying goes, "walk a mile in my shoes".

I don't have a magic wand to hand to you to make your debts disappear; if that is what you are looking for, the blunt reality is that there isn't an easy way to achieve it without a radical reordering of your thoughts, habits and attitudes. Getting out of debt requires more effort than doing nothing about the problem, but it is a problem that is very likely to get much worse in the future if you do nothing about it. You could dream of winning the lottery in order to make your debt problems disappear but the odds of winning the jackpot are about 45 million to one, so the brutal truth is that it is an extremely elusive dream. One of the ways in which it seduces you is the carrot dangled before you of 'someone is going to win it', and the belief that it plants in your mind that it is going to be you. That belief is just one of those subtle ways to get you to part with your money; the vast majority of people who participate in the lottery regularly will have spent far more than they have won. In the days before the lottery people used to say that they wished for 'a long-lost uncle to die and leave me a fortune' – but did you ever hear of that happening to anyone?

Interest rates are currently at their lowest in my lifetime and borrowing is relatively cheap at the moment, so now is the perfect time to get rid of debt before your borrowing becomes a lot more expensive. This period of cheap lending is not going to last forever and there are so many possible unexpected scenarios that could knock the global economy sideways; take the 2008 crash based on sub-prime mortgages for example, the population at large didn't see that one coming. If you do nothing, you may find a few years from now that your debt might become a far greater burden than it already is. Having a burden of debt now could leave you in a very vulnerable position in the future.

The journey ahead requires all the determination and discipline that you can muster, but reaching the destination in the journey to become debt-free is ample reward. I saw the journey towards freedom from debt as a punishment at first but looking back, the reality is that it is a huge opportunity with ample rewards that teaches you important lessons about yourself, your attitudes towards money and about life itself. You re-educate your attitudes to money and spending and it liberates you. It is exciting to take the journey from red to black and see your debts disappear and your savings increase. It is like making the effort to walk up a mountain; it looks daunting when you look up at the summit in the distance, but you take it one step at a time and once you get to the summit the view is amazing. The shift in changing your habits and attitudes about money is hard at first, but you will find over time that it becomes second nature and you will never want to go back to your old ways again. The choice lies before you – do you want the dark hole that you are stuck in to get deeper, or is it time to start carving out footholds that will help you to get out of the hole and back into the sunshine?

Chapter One

My story - how I got into a mess of debt

There is scarcely anything that drags a person down like debt.

- P.T. Barnum

I am a baby boomer, born to parents who lived through the Second World War and married in the 1950s. My parents had lived through rationing and hardship through the war, and started their married life as Britain's prosperity years were starting to take off. I had a fairly happy and comfortable upbringing in a good neighbourhood on the edge of town, spending many hours exploring the surrounding countryside by bike with my friends.

The pivotal decade of my upbringing was the 1970s when I made the transition from childhood to adolescence. It saw industrial unrest, terrorism and an oil crisis, but being young these events didn't really have much of an impact or make much of an impression on me. To me it was the glittery, glossy decade of glam rock and disco and the dawn of discount air travel that turned fantasy holidays, previously out of reach for many, into a reality. We had family holidays to destinations in continental Europe whilst many of my school friends still had holidays within Britain. There was no security screening in the first few flights I took (though the hijackings of the early 1970s were soon to lead to its introduction) and pilots would invite the children on board to come and see the cockpit. One memory that has never left me is from visiting the cockpit on a night flight and seeing the breathtaking beauty of the curvature of the earth in the distance. You had a lot more legroom on the planes; flying was pleasurable back then, but I don't enjoy flying any more. Back in the 1970s I dreamed of crossing the Atlantic but it seemed a distant dream, though later in life I was to make trips to the United States and Barbados.

It was a comfortable life but I always wanted more, especially in my early teens when the clothes that I wore were more important to me as I wanted to look fashionable. I was a rather gauche, introverted teenager with a tendency to tactlessness but with an aching desire to fit in amongst my peers. It was difficult when I got a place in a grammar school when I was eleven years old, as it was an all-girls' school and some teenage girls do have the unfortunate tendency to be bitchy and cruel. I think that one of the worst things that my father said to me in my childhood (and he said it often) was "Your schooldays are the best days of your life". I went through my adolescence in a state of mild depression (and you had to grin and bear it back then, there was no counselling and you just had to 'get on with it'), thinking that if these are the best years of my life, I'm really going to hate the rest. We wore uniforms to school but we often socialised at weekends and I wanted to look fashionable in order to fit in, but my mother kept me on a very tight clothes budget. When I was 14 I started to work at the weekends, firstly as a waitress and then a year later I worked in a supermarket. Nearly all my wages were spent on clothes and music.

I was fascinated by travel; in hindsight I realise that my parents had sacrificed a lot of other things to allow us to have foreign holidays, but I didn't realise that at the time. I longed to be an air hostess (though that's not a term that is used any more, it's now cabin crew member) which wasn't a good career choice as I was introverted, not very diplomatic and panicky in a tight spot; that wasn't exactly the character that was needed in the job. We didn't have good careers guidance back then, a careers advisor visited the school once and if you weren't interested in Oxbridge, she wasn't interested in you. I read as much as I could on the airline industry, even writing to the major airlines for their career literature and I concentrated on learning languages at school. I realise now that being cabin crew is hard work and very demanding, but I didn't see that; I was thrilled at the prospect of massive discounts for personal travel. I had grown up with seeing exotic places in movies and I longed to visit them. My parents had a newspaper delivered daily and it had celebrity gossip, some of it focusing on their exotic holiday destinations and one of my greatest desires was to travel to New York on Concorde. I did have a rebellious spirit though, only putting effort into subjects that interested me and my schoolwork suffered. I got 5 mediocre O Level passes when I was 16, the only good grade being in French. Fortunately I gained passes in English Language and Maths, as having these was a prerequisite for most clerical jobs at that time. The next step was sixth form college to study A Levels, but I didn't enjoy it and I left after six weeks.

Britain was now entering a recession and looking for work was difficult. After a few months I saw an advert for a Youth Opportunities Scheme post in a travel agency, I applied and got it with a weekly wage of £23.50 per week. Unfortunately I was in an all-female office that had echoes of the bitchiness of school and I hated it, and it also put me off my old dream of working for an airline. When it ended I decided to return to a Further Education college to do a secretarial diploma with A Levels. It was the syllabus inclusion of A Levels that appealed to me most and one of the options was French, my strongest subject; of the secretarial element I found that learning to type was useful but I couldn't get on the rest, especially shorthand. My longhand was always faster. We also had a principal teacher for our course whose main career advice was to use our secretarial work to access places where we would stand a chance of meeting someone rich and marrying well. At the end of the course I had acquired four more O Levels and two A Levels as well as scraping a pass for the secretarial certificate, and I started to look for work. I had recently passed my driving test and bought a car with an inheritance that had been bequeathed to me, a three-year-old Ford Capri. That horrified my father who tried to persuade me to get something sensible like a Mini, but I was determined to blow all my money on my 'poor man's Porsche', as one of my friends called it.

To have a job that was different appealed to me and it came a month after the end of my course in an advertisement for a job on the railways. It was the first job that I applied for and I was successful out of a field of fifty applicants. It was fortunate that I had bought the car as I would need it to get to work for very early shift starts. My starting salary was £4177 per annum and there was additional pay for compulsory weekend working. I was delighted when I got my first pay slip - £280! Nevertheless, by the time my next wage went in I had overdrawn on my bank account as I had gone on a spending spree.

I was earning a lot of money the following year as I did a lot of overtime, but I saved very little of it. I got married a year later and we bought a small house; we didn't have a deposit for it but we managed to arrange an endowment mortgage. Our mortgage repayment was £125 per month, which was about 10 per cent of our net earnings; it was a time when house prices were much more affordable. We started our married life living the good life; we would eat out regularly, bought new furniture, had frequent shopping trips and had a foreign holiday every year. Unfortunately neither of us applied a brake to our spending and we only saved sporadically for specific things. I had two credit cards, an Access card (the forerunner of MasterCard) and a Barclaycard, but I paid the balance in full every month. I managed to pay it off in full each month for three years until there was one month when I realised that I had spent so much on it that I couldn't afford the full payment, and that started the downward spiral of paying the minimum most months. I also kept getting increases in my credit limit every now and then, allowing me to spend more.

One big benefit of working for the railways was that I was entitled to ten free passes per year, each pass allowing me 48 hours of free rail travel, and I did use all of them up each year. I also got free or reduced price travel in many other countries and also on Sealink crossings and London Underground. One year we had a holiday in the south of France by rail that was very reasonable, for the travel element we only had to pay port taxes and the couchette berth fees. I once went on a three hour journey each way to Exeter for the day one Saturday because I had never been there before, and whenever I was feeling fed up I could catch the London train that left twenty minutes after the end of my shift in order to spend the afternoon in the capital. The frequent London trips were not altogether a good thing; I had expensive tastes and would visit shops like Laura Ashley, Liberty and Harrods.

After a few years on the railways I was successful in obtaining a Civil Service job as an Administrative Officer. It paid slightly less than my railway pay but they held an internal exam for promotion to Executive Officer two months after I had taken up the post; I went through the process and was successful. Just four months into my new employment, I was now earning more than in my previous job. The downside was that I was now working in the centre of a big city and that gave me more opportunities for spending.

A few years after I had started working there, disaster struck when my husband was made redundant; it was at a time of another economic downturn and it would be another six months before he found a job. We just about managed to stay afloat in that time as we had not yet reached the critical moment where our level of debt was unsustainable and I had plenty of overtime. Nevertheless, it was a struggle and we had to rein in our expenditure considerably. At one point when I could not balance the books, my mother gave me a lifeline by writing a cheque to cover the shortfall for that month. My mother would also meet me in town once a week for lunch and then to go round the market to buy me some fruit and vegetables for the week. Had we built up some savings we would have managed that period far more comfortably.

The job that my husband eventually found was low-paid and unsatisfying, and he decided that he would go to college to do a two-year computing course. In those days students had grants rather than loans. He started the course in September and also found a factory production job for four evenings per week, bringing our finances on an even keel again. At the end of the course he had obtained excellent marks and his tutors persuaded him to further his education by taking a degree course. He changed his part time job to work part time for a printing firm, and he went to work for them full time as a shift supervisor once he had completed his degree.

During these years there had been about three occasions when we had cut up our credit cards and had managed to reduce our debts. We didn't cancel the cards though, and I could still use them for mail order shopping so that added a bit of debt onto the bills. As we hadn't cancelled them, every time that the cards expired we received new cards and the cycle of overspending would start again. At regular intervals we would be notified of an unsolicited increase to our credit limits.

I had been promoted once more and we made the decision to move to another part of England. I obtained a transfer to another department and I met up with a former colleague who had moved up there previously; she was about to rent her home as she was moving away temporarily, so she offered it to me for six months at a reasonable rent so that I could look for a house to buy.

Even with our buoyant wages, maintaining two homes for four months strained our finances. Our credit cards at that time had quite low balances but it took four months for the sale of our house to go through and the expenses of commuting back home every weekend for four months mounted up. Our credit card bills started to rise again. We loved living in our new home; we went for regular hikes at the weekend in the wild and stunning countryside, beautiful beaches were close by and I made some good friends. Unfortunately I came to hate the office where I worked as I discovered that it had some longstanding management problems and a great deal of festering resentment. It took my husband two years to find work, during which time he did a long round trip commute every week to do four night shifts at the printing firm, but he was not to find a job that he could settle in and he had a succession of unsatisfactory and low-paid jobs. Even though I was still able to get a fair amount of overtime, our credit cards and loans had risen dramatically and three years after buying the house we took out a second mortgage of £50,000 to consolidate our debts, which we were able to do as house prices were rising and we had sufficient equity in our house.

After vowing never to get in such a financial mess again, we did little to change our spending habits and our debt was rising again. We decided that, as we didn't have children and had no-one to leave the house to after we died, why not rent instead? We took the decision to make a big downshifting and move away, and I would take the opportunity to study for a degree at a small university in a rural town. We sold our house and had the equity proceeds of about £30,000; after paying off our debts we had £10,000 left. We immediately put £6,000 of that into ISA accounts.

We had found a house to rent for £400 per month, a vast difference from our £1,200 per month mortgage payments, but it proved to be a difficult transition for me to go to a student loan income of £3,000 from a much higher salary. My husband only found low-paid work at first too; I had planned to get a part time job, but we arrived in the town just as the two major employers for part-time student jobs were closing down. We also found that there were amenities that we were used to that we couldn't find in the small town where we lived – previously we had always lived near a city – and we ended up having long drives for shopping trips to larger towns. I became disillusioned with the course too; I started the second year but left in November. I managed to find a full time job, but it was low-paid. We were starting to feel fed up about being stuck in the middle of nowhere, and looked at ways of moving back to civilisation.

All our savings had gone and our credit card debts were rising again, but they were manageable. Then out of the blue, disaster struck.

Chapter Two

The IVA – the end of a lifestyle of debt

Seek freedom and become captive of your desires. Seek discipline and find your liberty.

- Frank Herbert

I received the terrible news that my beloved mother was diagnosed with a terminal illness. She was very ill and needed constant nursing care, so I arranged a place at an excellent nursing home for her.

My employer was very understanding and gave me a lot of leeway to have long weekends. I then spent the next few months making a very long round trip every other weekend to visit her; the cost of fuel and paying for accommodation was enormous on my low salary, but I felt that I had limited time to spend with my mum and I wanted to make the most of it. They were happy times, though bittersweet with the knowledge of my mum's limited time left in this life; we talked a lot and I took her out in her wheelchair to go shopping several times. I will never forget mum's dignified attitude towards death; she was fully aware that her condition was terminal, but she was fearless about it and after she died the nurses told me how touched they were by her courage and dignity in the face of impending death.

Nevertheless, the toll of those months was great; the travelling was exhausting and it seemed like I had no spare leisure time at all. All my annual leave had gone on creating long weekends. I had to deal with the NHS, who had assessed her for end of life funding of her nursing home fees, and I was furious when I was later told in a circumspect way that the record of her assessment "was not available". In other words, they had lost it. After threatening to sue them should my mum die before the assessment took place, they reassessed her within days and they said that she was clearly eligible for funding as she was very ill indeed. It was a battle and a lot of wasted time and effort that I did not need at that time though.

My mother died about a week after that assessment; all the stress of travelling was over, but when I took stock of our finances we were maxed out on our credit cards and overdraft. We were broke. All our debts – excluding my student loan – totalled about £48,000. I had called a benefit fund that I had contributed to through my payroll to see if they could contribute even a small sum to keep us afloat. The first thing I was asked after I had briefly explained the situation was "Do you have children?" and when I said that I didn't, the answer was a flat no.

My husband and I realised that we had no choice but to tackle the problem, and we discussed an advert that we had seen in the paper of a debt management company. With a heavy heart, I decided to call them and when I sat by the phone, I had a flood of all the feelings I had felt throughout the years over the mismanagement of our finances. I felt humiliated, ashamed, and a failure. I got a sense of what it must have been like to be in the village stocks in past times, facing a crowd ready to pelt rotten eggs and mouldy cabbage leaves at you.

It turned out to be a far less painful experience than I had feared; I spoke to a man who ran through my options pragmatically and without judgement once I had explained my situation. I was set against bankruptcy as an option as I feared that anyone that I knew might read the bankruptcy notices in the local paper, so I felt that the best option would be to enter into an Individual Voluntary Arrangement (IVA) which would last for five years. He then said that he would arrange for an information pack to be sent to us so that we could decide whether to proceed.

With hindsight, now that I have learned more about debt solutions, it was not surprising that the man that I spoke to was so pleasant. Debt management companies are profit-making businesses and they make money from administrating IVAs and bankruptcies. When I received our closure report once the IVA was finished, the report stated that the firm had retained over £8,000 for its fees and expenses. It is not in their interest to suggest alternative ways such as approaching creditors to arrange a repayment schedule and this is an option that could have been explored had I gone first to a not-for-profit organisation such as Citizens Advice. I was mentally exhausted at that point though and close to a breakdown, with no energy to do some thorough research. That month my doctor signed me off work for two weeks with bereavement stress, and I took the opportunity to have a course of six counselling sessions through my employer's medical scheme.

The IVA pack arrived; we read through it, discussed it and decided to sign the papers and proceed. The way it worked was that we would list all our essential expenses, we would also be allowed £50 for contingencies, and the difference between that and our net salaries would be paid into the IVA. We would not be allowed to have a bank overdraft for the five-year duration of the IVA, or to enter into any lending; to breach this condition would lead to the failure of the IVA and that would lead to the company entering us into bankruptcy proceedings. The IVA would also show up on our credit records for one year after the completion of the IVA – though this was not a problem for us, we were never borrowing money again. Our research before signing the papers had spurred us into opening a 'parachute' account with another bank, seeing as the overdraft with our current bank was included in the IVA. Opening a bank account once the IVA was in place would have been difficult, as it would show up on our credit record.

It seemed a long, hard slog ahead – five years! During that time we cut our expenditure back dramatically; we had the occasional day out instead of holidays, we bought second-hand where possible instead of new, we would cook more and takeaways were very rare treats. The bottom line was always "Do we need it?" and we even found that we could save the contingency allowance in order to cope with unexpected emergency expenses. Once the car needed a big repair costing £600, and having the savings helped as we could pay it straight away and not be without transport as we lived in a small village. Sometimes it was close-run to keep in the black; once, the day before our pay went in the bank, we had a bank balance of six pence. We were allowed to miss a maximum of three payments during the IVA (any missed payments are tagged on to the end of the duration), which we did only once just after we had moved, two years into the IVA. We had another house move to a more prosperous area, where house rental was more expensive but we earned more as it was a high wage area. Luckily we found a house rental without going through an agency and the landlord did not do a credit check; we might have been turned down if he had, even though we had always paid the rent on time in our previous home. We hired a self-drive van in order to do the house removal ourselves and then we packed the remainder into the car.

Finally the slog ended, and we made our last payment nearly two years ago. A couple of months later we had cause to celebrate as we received the closure reports in the post; the end was now in writing and official. I still had a student loan debt from my disastrous attempt to study and I wasn't able to make additional payments in the duration of the IVA. Initially my earnings were under the threshold so I made no payroll payments for a couple of years and the total that I owed increased due to the interest that was added. In my next job I was earning slightly more, but my repayments made only a slight dent in the total that I owed. Since the IVA's end I have concentrated on paying it off and I now have only a small amount outstanding that will be paid off very soon.

It was difficult to face up to the hopeless situation that we were in and it had a big emotional toll as bankruptcy had always been a big fear for me but I faced it, dealt with it and triumphed. I hated having to account for our expenditure in the yearly review; it was as if there was someone watching over you all the time, but it did teach us the discipline that we so sorely needed to live within our means. With hindsight it's possible that an IVA wasn't the best solution for us, but it forced us into clearing the debt and to change our spending habits. All our previous efforts, cutting up our credit cards and vowing to get rid of our debts, had come to nothing. The greatest lesson throughout the five years and which is still ingrained in us today is to live within our means. We spend mainly in cash these days as it is easier to see how much you have left and it is not possible to overdraw this way. We still don't have a bank overdraft arrangement and we have not applied for any form of credit since the end of the IVA. It's been liberating and fun in a way to be creative in finding ways to curb our expenditure and save money, and I'll share some of those tips later.

Chapter Three

The state of Britain today – and how it used to be

The past is a foreign country – they do things differently there.
- L.P. Hartley, *The Go-Between*

Britons are overspending and overborrowing, and this has been steadily increasing each year since the 1970s. This statistic complements a society where its people feel insecure, alienated, lonely and fearful. We'll take a brief look at the state of Britain today and how it has altered in the half-century of my life, as I believe that the uncertainties and insecurities in modern life have a direct link to debt and overspending. I remember a time when housing was affordable for many and jobs were far more stable in most employment sectors than today. The 1970s witnessed the rise of large retail outlets that led to the loss of many small and long-established businesses and the decline of Britain's manufacturing base. Sadly, in parallel with this there has been a decline in the character of the British; to me they now seem to be more materialistic, superficial, vulgar, self-centred, aggressive and dishonest, and less compassionate, self-reliant, polite, rational and considerate. There seems to be a lack of a sense of honour and fundamental decency in too many people today.

The advantage of getting older is that you have a clear memory of how things used to be, 30 or 40 years ago, that cannot be conveyed fully by reading about it in a history book. Younger people living in today's society know no different from what they presently see around them. The society in my youth certainly wasn't perfect; in those days attitudes were expressed openly and without challenge that were sexist, racist and homophobic and I certainly don't want to see a return to that. There was however a more stable life for most people that I remember clearly, until the credit boom arrived in the 1980s.

The workplace

When I left school in the early 1980s it was fairly easy to enter the public sector and these jobs were considered to be jobs for life, unless you did something like punching your boss in the face. The requirement was usually five O Levels (the predecessors of GCSEs), including English and Maths. Today there are fewer public sector jobs, and that makes it is difficult to be successful unless the applicant has at least A Level qualifications and even graduates now apply for entry level administrative jobs. Computerisation had not yet reached the clerical sector and much record keeping was manual, so it was a labour-intensive occupation. I remember seeing an early word processor when I was at a Further Education college in the early 1980s, it was about the size of a wardrobe; the college only had the one word processor and typing students learned on manual typewriters.

Work contracts were mainly permanent; temporary contracts were to become an ever-increasing feature of the workplace towards the end of the decade and zero hour contracts were unheard of. You could happily enter into a mortgage contract knowing that you could depend on your salary. The Thatcher years saw a colossal shake-up of the public sector as many public institutions were privatised and the ones that remained saw the introduction of reduced budgets, so they became accountant-led. I saw the workplace become gradually far more stressful over the years as the drive to increase productivity became a priority and there was a greater emphasis on monitoring and appraisal. In the later years there was the mantra of 'embracing change' but it seemed to me that many managers were pressured into making changes for the sake of it rather than the necessity of change, simply to present a Brownie point at their appraisal. Change for no apparent reason led to a lot of stress on workers; people generally prefer stability to change and it was unnerving and stressful to become accomplished in a job but then be presented with a raft of new procedures and practices to learn. It is now a common interview question to be asked about how you adapt to change and I would suspect that many interviewees respond enthusiastically in order to get the job but secretly detest change. As the old saying goes, "If it ain't broke, don't fix it". Another management favourite is 'work smarter, not harder', which usually means that they are going to dump twice as much work on you than before and if you can't cope with it, it's your fault for being so disorganised.

The past fifteen years have seen a significant increase of workers who earn the minimum wage. In 1999, one in 50 employees were paid the minimum wage, but now it is one in 20[1]. Food banks are reporting that with rising housing costs some people in work are earning so little that they are forced to turn to food banks in order to survive.

Housing

In the mid-1980s we bought our first home with a 100% mortgage and the repayment was about 10% of our take-home pay. Today, owning a home seems well out of reach for young people and rents are also at an extortionate level in what has recently become the second most populated country in Europe, and the population is rising too. It is not only the young who suffer, as others may find themselves dropping out of the housing market in mid-life through calamities in their lives such as a relationship breakdown, ill health or loss of their job. Social housing is now severely restricted due to the introduction of Right to Buy legislation that put the majority of social housing into private hands and restricted funds to build new social housing even though there is great demand for it.

At the start of the 20th century a tiny minority of people -mainly aristocrats - owned most of the land in Britain but a booming population led to more landowners selling their land for house building. Better wages, more house building and the expansion of cities and industry saw a steady increase in home ownership. In the past decade, as more well-off people have entered the Buy to Let market and have pushed up house prices as a consequence, home ownership is starting to decline as we see a 'new aristocracy' of people with large property rental portfolios.

---

[1] http://www.theguardian.com/society/2015/oct/01/number-of-uk-workers-on-minimum-wage-expected-to-double-by-2020

Television programmes such as *Homes under the Hammer* annoy me, they may seem to be harmless entertainment but those properties sold at auction are mainly those repossessed by lenders, and it follows people making a quick buck on the back of the misery of the people who have lost their home. Why not make a programme that helps people on low incomes to obtain affordable housing?

It seems ridiculous that alternative housing solutions are not considered other than the traditional brick and mortar house build, and I suspect that the reason for this lies with the power of the construction industry lobby of parliament. Pre-fabricated houses are becoming more popular in other countries; they are much improved in comparison to Britain's post-war prefab houses and would provide a far more affordable solution. There also exists in Wales the right to live in a caravan on your own land or on land where you have permission to keep it, but England has strict (some say draconian) planning permission laws that prevent living permanently in a caravan in most cases.

Rental laws in Britain are also far more weighted to benefit the landlord than is the case elsewhere in Europe. Over the Channel you get a longer guaranteed tenancy that provides you with more security about your future; for example in Italy, the law guarantees a minimum four year tenancy from the landlord, but the tenant can end the tenancy earlier with a required period of notice. You can treat it to a greater extent as if it were your own home; minor alterations are allowed and you can keep pets in the property in most cases, even in flats. (For some strange reason many Italian rental properties don't have the kitchen installed, the tenant provides their own and I guess that it moves with them from home to home. I have no idea why that is, but most Italians are great cooks so maybe they are particular about their kitchen.) Many continental European countries have laws that impose a cap on rent increases, so they haven't seen the phenomenal rise in rents that has occurred recently in Britain.

So that is the situation that many people find themselves in, especially young adults; they cannot afford to buy as so much of their disposable income goes towards paying expensive and ever-increasing rent. There seems little will in parliament to address this problem, but that may be due to a significant number of MPs who own rental properties. There is also little coverage in the mainstream press on the plight of people on low incomes and the housing shortage; on the contrary, it seems that in recent years they have been actively promoting the idea of buy to let mortgages as an investment. A society that cannot house its people is a failed society.

Banking

In the 1970s, the branch bank manager knew his or her customers. You saw the manager if you wanted a loan or mortgage, but nowadays you are rarely likely to meet your bank manager. The banks encouraged financial prudence and you didn't get a flood of mail through your letterbox regularly enticing you to get credit cards and personal loans with them.

All that changed in the 1980s with the explosion of more readily available credit and the increased clamour from company shareholders for greater dividends. The banks were under pressure to lend more at interest – which is how banks earn their profits, there are no profits from customers who keep their accounts in the black and don't pay interest or charges – in order to compete with other lenders and to keep their share prices buoyant. It also saw the introduction of the Payment Protection Insurance (PPI) scandal that left thousands of lenders with insurance policies that in a lot of cases were worthless.

The banks don't lend you cash; they create the money that you receive by tapping numbers into a computer screen. In days of old, if someone agreed to lend you money at interest, the lender would hand over a bag of money or banknotes and the borrower would pay this money and interest back in cash by the agreed date. Nowadays there is a system called fractional reserve banking. Put simply, the bank has reserves of cash, and it lends out more cash than it physically holds based on a percentage of its cash reserves. It used to be that by law the proportion of reserves was 15 per cent; so for every £15 that the bank held, it could lend £100 on the strength of that £15. It then receives the loan repayments, of the sum lent plus interest, through the payments from your wages. Nowadays there is no legal minimum of the reserve, but it is in the interest of the banks that their fractional reserve is not too low; if a panic arose and everyone wanted to withdraw their cash from the bank, it would cause a crash as the banks would run out of money. Even if you want to withdraw a large amount in cash from your account, say £5,000, you now have to give your bank advance notice so that they don't run out of money at the branch that day.

So in a nutshell, you hand over money from your wages in instalments to pay off money that didn't exist in the first place; the banking system is creating money. The same is true with credit cards, which are another major earner for lenders through customers who do not repay the full amount each month and whose interest rates are much higher than the Bank of England base rate. A report in The Mail stated, "Justin Modray, founder of consumer advice website Candid Money, said: 'Credit card companies have grown very rich off the back of many customers not really understanding that making only the minimum payment can result in a huge debt.'"[2]

That is why banks and other lenders push so hard for you to take unsecured credit; it increases their profits and drives up their share price through your repaying them money that didn't exist in the first place.

The rich get richer and the poor get poorer

The gap between rich and poor has widened phenomenally; it was reported in 2015 that the richest people in Britain had doubled their wealth in the previous decade[3]. Where has that wealth come from? One of Britain's most significant sectors in the economy is the financial and banking sector and the economy's severe slump in 2008 due to the sub-prime mortgage scandal illustrated how central the finance businesses are in Britain's economy, and how dependent the country's trade balance is on its

---

[2] www.thisismoney.co.uk/money/cardsloans/article-3312716/Are-free-credit-cards-fuelling-addiction-debt-Borrowing-6-year-61bn.html

[3] http://uk.businessinsider.com/sunday-times-rich-list-2015-top-25-richest-people-uk-2015-4

fortunes. It is especially central now that Britain's industrial base is a pale shadow of its former self. The financial institutions played a large part in the fortunes of the rich as their share dividends went to its shareholders – whilst these include large institutions such as pension funds, they also include the rich. We have seen how their profits expand through consumer lending, and it is in their interests that the population continues to borrow excessively.

One aspect of the 1980s was the rise of Lord Hanson, a favourite of Margaret Thatcher. He was known as an 'asset-stripper'; he would buy what he felt were undervalued companies and make them profitable by making workers redundant and axing departments that did not produce a short-term profit, such as research and development. He was quoted as saying that his priorities were "shareholders, followed by customers, with employees coming last"[4]. His methods increased the share prices of his companies, setting a benchmark for other companies that wanted their shares to look healthy, but the cut of research and development harmed British industry in the long term as it hampered its ability to create new technology and products for the future. This obsession with share prices and quick returns is still with us in investment markets today – shareholders expect a large return in a short period of time.

We have also seen recently a glimpse of the extent of tax evasion by the rich with the release of the 'Panama Papers', the leak of papers listing clients of the Panamanian company Mossack Fonseca that hid money offshore for their rich clients. Rich people have

---

[4] http://pendientedemigracion.ucm.es/info/jmas/f&a/tiburon.htm

the resources to do this, as they are able to employ the best accountants, lawyers and tax advisers, and they also benefit from low-cost mortgages and other lending as they are considered low risk. The impact of this on the rest of the population is that the burden of taxation falls on lower income earners, who are also subsidising the lower interest rates of rich people's borrowing.

The 1980s saw the rise of the 'yuppie', the rich Young Upwardly-mobile Professional, and the film Wall Street was released in 1987 with its well-known quote "Greed is good". It also saw a surge in homelessness as the recession hit and public expenditure was drastically cut. In the previous decades we occasionally saw tramps, or 'gentlemen of the road'; they were usually old men, shabbily dressed, carrying a couple of bags with all their belongings and were often harmless and pleasant when they spoke to you. Major cities undoubtedly had their share of people sleeping rough, but smaller towns and cities saw little homelessness until the 1980s. Before the Thatcher era councils were better able to provide emergency accommodation to people who were homeless, but the effects of the recession saw many redundancies and council spending cuts meant that homeless people had fewer options for finding help. Homelessness has not been satisfactorily tackled to this day, and there seems little inclination from the population at large to exert political pressure to do so. I suspect that many see the homeless as undeserving people in a predicament of their own making, forgetting that the homeless are first and foremost people. I used to chat to a homeless man on my way to work and would buy him tea and spare him some change; he was a sweet and gentle man in a desperate situation.

In an age where attendance at Christian churches is in a decline in tandem with an age of a decline in community spirit and an increase in self-interest, church organisations have been at the forefront of alleviating the plight of the poorest people in Britain. They were the initiators in setting up food banks, and the organisation Church Action on Poverty encourages churches to run debt support groups and to create groups that foster a sense of local community and support.

In addition to the financial plight of the poorest members of society, they are largely ridiculed in the media and they have come to be despised by Britain's more prosperous citizens. It is true that there are some amongst the poor who are bad-mannered and unlikeable people but I have also met people like that who are much richer; you find them in all levels of society. Think of TV shows such as *Undercover Benefits Cheat* and *Benefits Street* to name a couple. These programmes plant the thought in the public's mind that every benefit claimant is lazy and cheating the system, but the truth is that the figure lost to the Treasury through tax evasion is a far greater sum. According to Community Links:

"Benefit fraud is largely overestimated by the general public: in 2011/12 only 0.7 per cent of the benefit bill (equivalent to £1 billion) was overpaid due to fraud. Compare this to the £70 billion lost through illegal tax evasion and an entirely different story emerges. In fact, a recent IPSOS Mori survey found that the public tend to overestimate the extent of fraudulent claiming by a factor of 34 (only 70p of every £100 spent on welfare is claimed fraudulently, not the figure of £24 generally believed by the public)"[5].

This quote mentions tax evasion (which is illegal) but the rich are also in a position to engage in strategies of tax avoidance (which is legal). It is a controversial point that one is illegal whilst the other is not.

The poorest members of British society are also exploited by a financial system that considers them to be high-risk borrowers – and thus they are charged much higher interest than more well off borrowers, and the higher interest they pay subsidises the cheaper borrowing of others who are better off. Pressure from campaign groups has forced the government to make steps towards tackling the unethical lending practices of payday loans companies and doorstep lending.

What do we infer from all this?

In tandem with a burgeoning amount of personal debt, there is increasing uncertainly and instability in people's lives with regard to work, housing and money, which are the basis of a secure life – and I haven't even touched on other issues such as the spectres of terrorism and crime that unsettle many people. Possessions do make people feel secure, it may be that many feel the need to overspend on many things that they don't need in order to provide a cocoon for themselves from the pressures of modern life. I do believe that I had a simpler childhood than many young people today, and that my parents did

---

[5] http://www.community-links.org/linksuk/?tag=benefit-fraud

before me and my grandparents did before them – and that is despite all of them living through wars.

What I didn't have in my earlier life was so many distractions and so many bewildering choices; today we have an overload of information through much more advanced electronic media and retail choices are greater. Does more choice mean satisfaction though? If you have a satellite or cable service for TV, you might have over 1000 channels and most of it doesn't interest you, but it wastes a lot of time flicking through trying to find something worth watching. I have heard it said that two options is a choice, and more than two options is a dilemma. In addition to society's instabilities and uncertainties, contemporary life seems to be bewildering and overwhelming; this does not lend itself to a nation of well-balanced, pragmatic and sensible people. It is hardly surprising that there is a rise in flights of escapism and unhealthy attitudes towards spending.

Chapter Four

A culture that lures you to spend

The proximity of a desirable thing tempts one to overindulgence. On that path lies danger.
- Frank Herbert

Have you ever thought in any depth about the effect that popular culture has on you and those around you? Advertising is often annoying, sometimes amusing, sometimes erotic, but it's just some detail in the background – or is it? On a subconscious level your mind takes in everything. Following the lives of famous people is also a bit of harmless fun, isn't it? I think that many people look upon the rise of celebrity culture with unease and distaste, but feel that they are a tiny voice against a roar of popular culture. Have you wondered why people seem to be more emotional these days, sometimes exploding into rage if they don't get their own way, even if their demands are unreasonable? It is my view that these three elements of our society today are instrumental in the rise of consumerism and burgeoning personal debt.

The consumerism snare

Advertising is the art of arresting the human intelligence just long enough to get money from it.
- Chuck Blore

Advertising didn't sway me. I was a strong-minded, logical person and I was impervious to marketing strategies that induced me to spend, and I'm sure that many reading this will feel the same way. That's what I always believed, but once I started to research the subtleties of marketing and advertising and looked into how it seeps into so many areas of our lives, I believe that it is impossible to escape from the power of advertising unless you make a conscious effort to do so - and even then you will only lessen your exposure, unless you go to live in a cave. If you are exposed to advertising you are likely to be seduced by it. You see advertising on television, your computer, your phone, on any journey that you take, in magazines and newspapers; it infiltrates most areas of our lives.

The global expenditure on advertising in 2015 was projected to be $592.4 billion (approximately £409.35 billion)[1], so when you consider that there are about 7 billion people in the world, that is about £5 for each man, woman and child. Seeing as there are many people worldwide who are untouched by advertising as they live in remote areas, a large proportion of that expense is concentrated on the five largest advertising markets; the United States, United Kingdom, China, Japan and Germany. If you live in one of these five countries you face a barrage of advertising, and the reason why so much is spent on advertising is that it is effective. Advertising agencies engage in a significant amount of research in order to understand the psychology of the consumer; even the subtle use of

---

[1] www.emarketer.com/Article/Advertisers-Will-Spend-Nearly-600-Billion-Worldwide-2015/1011691

certain colours, images and phrasing of words contribute towards ads that hook you in.

Manufacturers have advertised their products for centuries, but previously there was an emphasis on the usefulness and durability of their products; it was an item that you needed and was built to last a long time. Before the early twentieth century everyone but the rich bought items mainly on the basis of need rather than desire. Modern marketing began with Edward Bernays (a nephew of psychologist Sigmund Freud), an American who had worked on propaganda for the government in World War One. After the war he thought about how to apply propaganda to peacetime, and he renamed it 'public relations' – what we now commonly call PR – because of the negative connotation of the work 'propaganda'. It will be very useful to you if, from now on, you substitute 'advertising' with 'propaganda' in your mind. For a more detailed analysis of his expansion of marketing I would recommend that you watch Adam Curtis' documentary *Century of the Self*, and you will hear Bernays' daughter recall that her father said to her that the masses were "stupid". He brought in a new form of advertising that led people into buying products on the basis of desire rather than necessity (in other words, things that they didn't need) as a way to bolster the profits of big business. The advertising aimed to appeal to consumers on an emotional level rather than a rational one and one of the tactics that he used was celebrity endorsement.

Bernays' early theories were based on his uncle's theories of crowd mentality and advertisers would question a sample of people about their preferences and see what the majority desired. They realised that the behaviour of consumers was not as reliable as the questionnaire results had predicted, so the 1950s saw the rise of the focus group where customers were invited to gather in a group and discuss what they thought about a product. The 1960s saw the rise of hippie culture, anti-establishment sentiment and the rise of individualism. Market researchers devised ways in which to entice the more individualistic members of society into consumer culture by focusing on the lifestyles and values of their consumers. They would research the lifestyles of their target consumer, for example to formulate marketing designed to appeal to young men, and tailor their advertising accordingly. It was found in the 1980s that individualism was becoming increasingly more central in Britain as well as in the United States and people were mainly concerned with satisfying their own desires.

I took part in a focus group once; I was approached in a newly-opened city centre supermarket and was asked if I could spare a couple of hours that evening to discuss the new supermarket branch, and for this I would be paid £30. I went to the focus group, which was being held in a meeting room in the best hotel in town and we were treated to sandwiches, cake and tea. It was an interesting couple of hours as we all discussed a wide range of questions about the store and the products that it offered. I thought later that it was a generous payment for a couple of hours and the venue rather extravagant, but I think that it is in human nature to want to give back in exchange for someone's generosity, so it was an ambience designed for us to share openly and freely without holding back.

Anyone who has lived through the 1970s and beyond can see that the media - especially television and magazines – has dumbed down considerably. In 1980 I watched the dramatisation *Death of a Princess*, which caused so much controversy that Saudi Arabia threatened to cut off diplomatic relations with Britain, but it was aired anyway. TV bosses would not have the courage to air such a programme today. I remember John Pilger's documentaries, especially about the atrocities in Cambodia and East Timor, and the BBC's *Play for Today* series that dramatised social and political issues. You no longer see such hard-hitting programming today, and the power of advertisers probably has a major part to play in this. Although the BBC is not a commercial channel, it has dumbed down its programming in response to the commercial channels that were capturing larger audiences. Advertisers have a say in where their adverts are placed and this places pressure on the TV channels and magazine publishers in the type of material that they produce, as Ben Bagdikan states:

"An article that put the reader in an analytical frame of mind did not encourage the reader to take seriously an ad that depended on fantasy or promoted a trivial product. An article on genuine social suffering might interrupt the 'buying' mood on which most ads for luxuries depend"[2].

So that is the reason why there is so much television programming that does little to stretch and improve your mind. You also will not see critiques of marketing techniques and how that leads to debt in

---

[2] Quoted in www.globalissues.org/article/160/media-and-advertising

the mainstream media as they rely so heavily on their advertising revenue, and the companies who are paying for adverts won't want to see any criticism of advertising. Watching television also induces a mild hypnotic state through the flickering of the screen, a state similar to deep relaxation, which opens up your suggestibility to advertising.

Have you ever read a book on marketing and sales techniques? I hadn't until very recently. I guess that you probably haven't either if you don't work in sales and marketing, but it is an eye-opener of how they hook you in on a subconscious and emotional level. I remember going to a cosmetics counter in a department store for one specific item; the sales assistant had a "Sales Assistant of the Year' certificate on display and that should have rung alarm bells for me. She drew me into a discussion on other products and offered to give me a hand massage whilst talking to me – oh, that massage felt so nice. I ended up buying the product I wanted, plus two other impulse buys due to the assistant's persuasion – all on my credit card. Relaxation puts you into a more suggestive mood, so that hand massage certainly worked to add to my debt.

According to the BBC programme Shop Well for Less, research on shopping decisions showed that 20% are made on a rational level, 40% on an emotional level and 40% on a habitual level. That means that logical thought and reason are behind only a fifth of our purchases. The programme showed that consumers believed that dearer branded labels were always better quality and that they bought certain brands out of habit, but when they used less expensive supermarket or high street own brands in a blind test, they often could not tell the difference. Supermarket own label products are often produced by the manufacturers of branded products anyway – the supermarkets don't have their own food and toiletries production factories. It is, however, the manufacturers who advertise their products whereas the supermarkets run ads for the brand of their shops as a whole, so it is therefore more likely that the specific items advertised by the manufacturers will remain in the memories of consumers. This is where brand loyalty is cultivated.

As advertisers know, sex sells. I remember when an upmarket American ice cream was being introduced to Britain. Its advertising showed scantily clad people eating ice cream in a highly provocative manner, which suggested that eating fat and sugar makes you sexy. It doesn't; it makes you fat. I still bought it, though. I have noticed that the most seductive advertising is shown in cinemas which, if you think about it, is the arena that grabs your whole attention. If you watch a film on television, your attention can be drawn elsewhere; the neighbour's dog barking, traffic noise, the phone might ring and you can do other things whilst you're watching such as checking your phone or ironing. In the cinema you are in the dark with no distractions at all; provided of course that you have a well-behaved audience and don't have some idiot near you who is holding a running commentary throughout the film and fishing for sweets at the bottom of a particularly crackly bag. The screen commands your complete attention and, sitting in your comfy seat, you are particularly open to suggestibility. Having a cinema-sized television screen in your house will help to induce this suggestibility too.

Celebrity culture: envy and desire

Glamour: deceptive or bewitching beauty or charm; mysteriously exciting or alluring physical attractiveness, especially when artificially contrived.
- Oxford English Dictionary

I have included the definition above in the hope that you will notice the words 'deceptive' and 'artificially'. If you like Terry Pratchett, I would suggest that you read (or reread) his novel *Lords and Ladies*; in my opinion he sets out perfectly the true nature of glamour.

Human beings are social creatures by nature and it is only natural to take an interest in other people. This has been satisfied mainly in the past by an interest in the lives of the people of the communities in which they lived; they shared the fortunes, good and bad, of those around them. If a family fell on hard times, their extended families and neighbours would pitch in to help. They would occasionally share gossip from outside their social circle that related to people higher up the social scale. With the growth of literacy and increased circulation of newspapers from the mid-nineteenth century, people were exposed increasingly to the trivia of the lives of the rich. The post-war years saw an increase in tabloid journalism, and today we see an interest in the lives of the rich that has turned into an obsession for many and they pay far less attention to the people around them them in their immediate surroundings.

I have seen an explosion of interest in celebrities in the past 30 years, fuelled by an increasing number of celebrity gossip magazines and the internet. In the 1970s, you wrote off to join a fan club. Now you can 'like', 'friend' or 'follow' your favourite celebrity which creates an illusion of even closer proximity to them and you can have constant updates on what they are posting. I do wonder if they really write their own posts; they just might employ a 'Social Media Consultant' to do it for them. Celebrities play to this imaginary cyber relationship and foster the illusion of the celebrity as your friend. There is no greater illustration of this than the outpouring of grief at a celebrity's death. Maybe the death of Diana, Princess of Wales had something to do with this present-day phenomenon, as before then people would feel a bit sad and maybe say what a shame it was at the passing of someone in the public eye, and that was all. Now it's common to see hundreds of social media comments along the lines of "OMG!!! I can't stop crying!" – and it's not even someone that they know personally. How would they cope with the death of a relative?

Perhaps the increase in individualism and egotism that we see in today's society has led to the need to escape what an individual sees as a boring life by obsessing about celebrities' lives; a way of vicariously leading an exciting life. I can understand this to a point; I used to daydream in my teen years about being rich, which I'm sure was an escape from the inadequacies that I felt in my life at that point. Words like routine, responsibility, order, discipline and prudence – and the concepts that they define - have become reviled and maybe there is a widespread flight to escapism in order to avoid facing life head-on. In tandem with this phenomenon there is increased social isolation and a loss of community spirit. There are people who care more about the lives of celebrities than the old lady a few doors down who may be struggling to survive.

A lack of compassion for the people around you is bad enough, but this obsession also gives people unrealistic aspirations and expectations as they see the route to celebrity fame as easy. Famous people who have made it to the top would tell you otherwise:

"Talent is cheaper than table salt. What separates the talented individual from the successful one is a lot of hard work." - Stephen King

"Movies are hard work. The public doesn't see that. The critics don't see it. But they're a lot of work. A lot of work." - Robert De Niro

"There are no secrets to success. It is the result of preparation, hard work, and learning from failure." - Colin Powell

"It's hard work making movies. It's like being a doctor: you work long hours, very hard hours, and it's emotional, tense work. If you don't really love it, then it ain't worth it." - George Lucas

Is the celebrity life of fame and fortune that many people crave the paradise that it's made out to be? I heard an interesting comment at a seminar I attended, the speaker was a magazine editor who encountered people from all walks of life. The conversation with the audience had turned to money, their lack of it and how better it would be to be rich, and she replied incredulously, "Do you think that rich people don't worry about money?" She expanded the comment by explaining that there is always someone richer than you; if you're a millionaire, there are still billionaires above you in the strata of wealth. She said that many rich people felt the need for ostentation, and were pressured into competing with their peers to obtain the best luxurious possessions. In the 1970s, it seemed that most celebrities travelled by scheduled airlines (first class of course) but now it seems that the pinnacle of success is the private jet. Even some celebrities who campaign on environmental issues use private jets, which is a tad bit hypocritical, don't you think?

During my teenage years, ordinary people did not expect to buy designer labels. Designer clothes were for people with a lot of money who could afford them; we bought our clothes at Chelsea Girl and Top Shop whenever possible but headed for the market stalls if we didn't have much to spend. Nowadays there seems to be an obsessive aping of the the rich in any way possible and even some young children crave designer labels. There is even a flourishing trade on eBay of carrier bags from designer stores such as Gucci and Prada; there's nothing in them, you just get the carrier bag, but you can then swan down the street carrying a designer store's carrier bag. Did you know that in the Middle Ages the law prescribed the types of clothing and jewellery that people could wear according to their wealth and social status? Maybe that wouldn't be such a bad thing today, as there would be no point in hankering after designer labels that you couldn't afford as you wouldn't be allowed to wear them. "But we have a right to choice!" I hear you cry; yes, the right to make choices that may be irresponsible and put you in a trap of debt. There is an old saying, 'If wishes were horses, beggars would ride', meaning that you can't have everything that you want, though 'beggars' nowadays reach for their plastic.

Celebrities are now marketed in the same way as any other product is marketed, and they are also paid millions to endorse products as their fans want to own the things that their favourite celebrities endorse. Think of perfumes and aftershaves as well – it amazes me when I cast an eye over perfume ranges and see so many that are named after celebrities. I don't remember a single celebrity perfume being on sale in my youth.

In case you believe that acquiring millions will be an end to your money problems, here are just some of the debts accumulated by some famous people:

Michael Jackson, singer – approximately $400 million at the time of his death
Annie Leibovitz, celebrity photographer – $24 million
Kanye West, singer - $53 million
Burt Reynolds, actor - $10 million

Celebrity is no guarantee that you will never get into debt, but the scale of it is far bigger – and more public.

Aside from money problems, celebrity interviews portray perfect lifestyles. Celebrities employ PR people to deliver this illusion though – in politics, it's known as 'spin'. Of course some of their problems don't remain hidden; you get to hear about the divorces, the drink-driving convictions and the journeys to rehab that manage to leak to the press. So what you mainly see is only what the celebrities want you to see and they project the image of a perfect life, and their problems largely stay hidden. Who is to say, if you came into a lot of money, that you wouldn't go from a poor and miserable existence to a rich and miserable one? I have met a few rich people in the past who were leading very unhappy lives. As for getting into a relationship with someone rich, that's highly unlikely to end your problems; I heard a saying once that "No-one works harder for their money than a woman who marries it". If that is what you desire, you will be up against more competition than you can ever imagine. A friend once had a date with someone well known; she told me that it was such an eye-opener for her, as she was constantly bombarded with attempts to elbow her out of the way by other women. That was just one date, too – can you imagine living like that all the time?

There is so much distorted identification with celebrities these days that some people think of their favourite celebrities as kindly, benevolent people; they don't realise that they are seeing an image and not what is below the surface. Some may truly be kind and benevolent, but you only see what they want you to see and to believe about them via their PR outlets - for all you know they may be the most nasty people who beat their kids and torture puppies for fun. You just don't know what goes on behind the veneer of perfection. It is an revealing to be in a job that exposes you to people from all walks of life, as I was when I worked on the railways. I encountered quite a few rich and famous people such as politicians, aristocrats and actors. Some were pleasant (I found the prison reformer Lord Longford to be delightfully charming), but quite a lot of them treated you as if you were something stuck to their shoe that they had trodden in. Even when their appalling behaviour does get reported in the media it doesn't seem to make much difference to their fans; a few years ago Justin Bieber was photographed on a balcony and spitting on his fans who had gathered below and for some unfathomable reason he still has a huge following.

Some celebrities like to focus on the charitable work that they do but I see few celebrities who focus their efforts on the problems in their own countries. I see nothing wrong with overseas charity work but I would argue to an extent that 'charity begins at home' and there is grinding poverty in Britain and the United States that few well-known people have the inclination to address. As we have seen, however, we have a culture that reviles the poor, and rich people who venture out with bodyguards and live in homes with tight security are insulated from the reality and the problems of the poor in their own country.

A distorted identification with a projected image can become an unhealthy obsession in some people and can also lead to stalking of their celebrity of choice; I think that it would be a life of hell not to be able to walk down the street unrecognised by people that I don't know personally and maybe to feel the need to hire bodyguards for protection; that's on top of wondering which of your friends are passing on gossip about you to the tabloids. Then there are the hangers-on who only seek out a celebrity's company for their fame. Give me anonymity and a normal life any day.

As with winning the lottery, people who crave fame often do not realise that the odds are stacked against them. Many are called, but few are chosen. The desire to appear on television has become an ever-increasing obsession. Consider this quote from a mother in the documentary *Starsuckers*; "A parent's best dream is to see their kid on TV." Parents used to want prosperity, good health and happiness above all for their children; now they are content to see their little darling's grinning face on TV for a few seconds and that's all their hopes fulfilled.

Everyone likes to have some recognition from others, but the decline of community participation and social isolation has led many to seek virtual relationships – or maybe vice versa, perhaps leading virtual lives has led to the weakening of community. You could say that social media such as Facebook is providing a measure of the attention that its users seek and is thus feeding into fame culture, with the number of friends and how many likes you can get for your posts as the measure of your popularity. The pinnacle of success is a post that goes viral. You can have interaction on a global scale through social media and any forum that appeals to you, but it creates relationships with little substance. Professor Robin Dunbar of the University of Oxford, in an interview for the documentary *Starsuckers* stated, "The brain is designed to handle face to face interaction, not virtual interaction".

I read recently that employers were complaining about the lack of social skills in their young applicants. Has the predominance of social media become so overwhelming that people are losing their skills to interact on a personal level? I find it sad that more people are craving fame and attention; we all want to be liked, though in my case I am happy to be liked by my circle of wonderful close friends and I don't have any desire to be adored by millions. It suggests to me that there is a deep malaise at the heart of many people today, and not only among young people, in that they crave satisfaction and recognition outside themselves. Seeking to be liked for your looks, how you dress and what you own indicate deep-seated psychological unease with one's core of identity.

So there you have my view on celebrity culture. Crazy, isn't it?

The New Age movement has a lot to answer for

What is loosely termed the New Age Movement mushroomed during the 1970s and beyond. In the 1990s I embraced it enthusiastically; it espoused values that were dear to me such as environmentalism, natural health and self-growth. I try to be a good person and I saw this route as a way to be kinder and seek better ways of living. I also spent a lot of money in the quest for self-realisation on books, workshops, courses and a lot of paraphernalia. It seems to me that the disillusion with and decline of Christianity in the West has left a spiritual void and lack of moral direction that many feel the need to fill, but I found that the 'spirituality-lite' of the New Age lacked depth and substance. In the middle of the last decade I had become disillusioned, the catalyst occurred after I met a couple of the big names and it was apparent that they were first and foremost business people whose aim was to get as much money from you as they could. I also learned later that quite a few of the key figures who were instrumental in starting the New Age movement had ties to the intelligence services, but that is another story. As we have seen that marketing strategies target lifestyles and values, you can bet that they have not overlooked the New Age lifestyle.

It also dawned on me that a lot of people that I met at various gatherings (mostly women, but not exclusively so) were intelligent people – the sort of people who would have marched on the streets in the 1960s and 1970s to protest at social injustices. I heard the message so often that we should not watch the news as "it is negative energy", so it succeeded in creating a class of people who had largely disengaged from social issues through embracing a superficial pseudo-religion. In other words, it was creating people who would be docile and would think that they were changing the world with their positive energy – though I would argue that all those positive vibes did nothing to prevent the awful global events since the start of this century.

Politicians have cottoned on to how the electorate were becoming more individualistic than community-minded; voters cast their vote on what they thought was the best deal for them as an individual. The socialism that my parents knew is now a thing of the past as the majority of people think of their own self-interest rather than the community as a whole; they like the idea of improving public services, as long as they don't have to pay for it. Embracing the New Age entails introspection, but that can go too far and it becomes navel-gazing, where you get so wrapped up in yourself that you do not see what truly matters around you.

Some things that I came across were bunkum but I haven't discarded all of what I learned in those fifteen years; some of it was useful. I did gain more strength of character, boldness and confidence that improved my self-esteem for the better. Meditation is scientifically proven to be beneficial to mental wellbeing, and I still do yoga that helps to keep me fit and keeps my joints in good shape. The downside was that it did lead me to aim to 'live for the moment' and to 'live my dream', culminating in the disastrous decision to leave my boring but well-paid and stable job to move to the middle of nowhere, a decision that I regret to this day. Ironically a year after I left that job I heard that the office was going to close and had I stayed, I would have had either a generous relocation package or a big redundancy payment.

It is my belief that New Age philosophy has helped to lead to the majority of people being at the mercy of their emotions rather than their logic, as I see the use of its themes and terminology increasing in mainstream society. There is nothing wrong with maintaining a positive mindset, though it is the nature of life that you have peaks and troughs in your life and you can't be happy all the time. It is far better to aspire to contentment than happiness; to be content with your life, with what you have and what you have achieved despite its hardships and challenges.

I think that the characters of my parents and grandparents enabled them to cope better with difficult times. The 'Dunkirk spirit' of the British people has become a hackneyed cliché, though I believe that the essence of strength of character that could cope with most hardship that came your way did exist in the generations before me. I saw this strength of character in my parents and grandparents, whose approach to their lives was solidly grounded in reality rather than illusion and desire. They didn't collapse into emotional wrecks (and they would rather have died than bare their souls on a TV show); they just got on with life as best they could, and they had a lot of hardships and challenges to overcome. My grandfathers served in the armed forces during the Second World War; one was posted to the Middle East and he didn't see his family for five years. In their lives there was however the support of the community and their extended families that has largely been lost in modern Britain; there was also the recent memory of poverty and fear of the workhouse that drove my ancestors to work hard and do well in life. I am aware that two of my ancestors died in the workhouse in the late 19th century, and that memory would have been carried forward in the family into the next century. Those memories are now becoming much dimmer, as is the memory of struggling through the war with food rationing. You see that ethos still in many Mediterranean countries today where there was widespread poverty throughout the 1950s as their war-torn countries struggled to recover. Many of their young people will have heard what life was like then from their grandparents. I still see in them today a desire to work hard, succeed and acquire material security – and a horror of incurring debt, even to buy a house, which they often prefer to do once they have saved up to buy a house outright. It is noticeable that their people are much more grounded, sensible and honest and there is a stronger and better sense of community. Their young people are often a lot more polite and respectful as well, especially towards the elderly. Maybe the dimming of the memory of abject poverty in Britain is a factor in the increase of consumer debt, the desire for a lifestyle that is unattainable for many and for increasing selfishness; is that how decadent Britain has become?

It now seems that many people believe that they have the right to be happy and to do whatever they want all the time, often dreaming of 'getting rich quick' without putting in any effort of their own. TV talent shows are very popular – I never watch them – and it may seem to viewers that talent alone can bring fame and riches easily, but many stars would tell you that they only achieved wealth and fame through overcoming setbacks along the way and through a considerable amount of hard work. There is a lot of material about that tells you about manifesting what you want; you just have to put the vibes out to the universe and what you desire will appear – you can manifest a Porsche, a dream home, a wad of money and a gorgeous partner into your life. Of course we are constantly being told that reality isn't real (as in the Matrix films, for example) – but physical reality is the only one I know, where you don't get anywhere without putting some effort in. Hard work is real in my physical reality. The only way that you are going to get rich through manifesting wealth practices is to write a book about manifesting wealth.

Let's just consider 'reality is an illusion' for a moment and look at it critically. Who is promoting this stuff, and are they trying to mess with our minds? Until recently people used to believe in a solid, material reality and maybe also a more ethereal existence where you went to once you departed this world, and in the main they were far more sensible and grounded. According to this theory of an illusory reality (and it is just a theory), a guy could stand in the middle of a railway track looking at a train hurtling towards him but don't worry, it's just an illusion. Whoops, he's dead. Don't worry about debt, it's just an illusion. Those threatening letters from your creditors are just an illusion. The notice to appear in court for non-payment of your debt – an illusion. Tell that to the judge.

So there is now the misguided feeling that wealth and recognition can come easily. What you don't get though, from getting all that you want easily without working hard for it and having the patience to wait for it, is appreciation. There is a deep satisfaction that is gained from getting something that required lot of effort and patience to attain. The persistence and determination to strive for a goal seem to be food for the soul – how can you appreciate that which is handed to you on a plate? I love the old saying 'clogs to clogs in three generations' (clogs were the footwear of the poor in the past, and better off people wore shoes), which also had a variant of 'wealth does not pass three generations'. It meant that someone may work their way out of poverty through hard work, their children would realise the value of hard work (and would thus have shoes), but the next generation would be spoilt and lazy, squander their inheritance and end up in poverty - and clogs.

One of the favourite New Age topics was the 'inner child', to free the hurt in the trapped memory of being a child within you. I was never comfortable with this as I have generally been satisfied with life as an adult. I do wonder if this has contributed to the phenomenon of the 'kidult' – the adult who doesn't grow up and remains interested in pursuits that were traditionally for children. The latest phenomenon is adult colouring books and I'm sorry if you enjoy your colouring books, but those are for kids. They teach children how to draw within lines as a way of developing art skills, but then you grow up and study art; adults would then go to an art evening class or join an art group, but of course that is more demanding and requires more effort. The rise of celebrity culture may well have had a part to play in the regressive nature of adults; it is a far easier pursuit to follow the lives of B-listers and fantasise about living their life than it is to read books, engage your brain and educate yourself. It is a way of escaping the challenges of life, but it is when you face and overcome your challenges that you learn and mature.

I would argue that traits of kidulthood are seen in a growing number of adults today. Why do so many people need escapism? Why are they regressing? Why do they feel that they can't cope with adult life? Is adult life truly perceived to be so boring? Above all, why don't they grow up? Is that too hard to do these days? I'm not suggesting at all that adults should be dullards. There is nothing wrong with being young at heart and having a sense of fun, but these need to be combined with responsibility and maturity. This phenomenon of kidulthood is far too excessive and unhealthy.

Conclusion

Though this chapter started with the topic of advertising, I feel that the influences of celebrity culture and of New Age thought have contributed significantly to our susceptibility to advertising and to desiring things that we don't need. As a whole they have led to a feeling of inadequacy in our lives and of dissatisfaction. Even if you have shunned New Age philosophy, its influence has been pervasive as we become more touchy-feely and emotional. Whilst you may think this is not a bad thing, it is prudent to remember that PR was invented as a form of propaganda and that there are many people and organisations out there who are happy to manipulate this change in society's values and divest you of your money. Desiring things that are far beyond your reach is an easy way to set out on the road to debt.

Chapter Five

Revise your spending

He who buys what he does not need steals from himself.

- Swedish proverb

So, what do you *need*?

I'll never forget one of the most ridiculously histrionic comments that I ever heard about spending. "I'll just die if I don't get that dress!" Just think about the stupidity of that statement for a moment, and it was especially stupid as it came from someone with a wardrobe that would stock a charity shop to the rafters. Will she keel over and her heart stop if she doesn't get it? No of course not, but it just illustrates how for some people 'wants' have metamorphosed into 'needs' and require instant gratification.

Put simply, your basic needs are:

- Shelter
- Food
- Heat

Those are your basic priorities. You need somewhere to live, sufficient calories and the right nutrition to keep your body functioning, and warmth when it's cold, either by heating your house and/or wearing sufficient clothes to keep the cold at bay. In addition to those basic needs, you might also need a car if you can't get to work by walking, cycling or public transport and you are not able to get a lift from someone else. You might also need to buy medication to recover from or control a medical condition.

Now that you realise how marketing has subtly influenced you into transforming your 'wants' into 'needs' and into overspending to the extent that you are in debt, you can start to look critically at your spending. Do you really need a cinema-sized television? A brand new car? New kitchen appliances when the ones you have still work? The latest fashions because someone is telling you what you should wear this autumn? To buy everything brand new instead of secondhand? So many clothes and shoes? Two weeks in the Seychelles?

We have all heard the expressions 'retail therapy', 'shopaholic' and 'when the going gets tough, the tough go shopping' and I have often heard these used in a positive and laudatory way, as if being a shopaholic is a badge of honour. Let's be clear about this, they are not positive; they are harmful attitudes and induce you to spend even more, which is damaging both to your finances and your self-esteem in the long run. Shopping is not 'therapy' – things that make you tangibly better and whole such as physiotherapy and counselling support are therapies. All that retail therapy will do is burden you with more debt and then harm your well-being as a result. There is a common error in the perception of the demographics of compulsive shoppers; there is a widespread preconception that they are women who buy far too many clothes and shoes, but men are equally capable of overspending, particularly on cars, electronic gadgets and power tools. Men have also become far more fashion-conscious than they were back in the 1970s and are now likely to spend more money on high-end clothes, skincare and hairdressing.

Keep a record of your spending

You won't have a clear idea of the extent of your spending unless you keep an account of it. Carry a notebook and pen with you and jot down everything you buy (recording what it is and what it cost), even the smallest expenditure, and add it all up at the end of the day. Make totals also for each weekly spend and then for your monthly spend. You need to keep doing your tally of spending every day as if you do it for a few days and then give up, you will have no idea of your level of spending.

Look critically at the list. How many of those purchases were impulse buys, and are you making unnecessary purchases on a regular basis because they don't cost much? If you spend £5 on things that you don't need daily over five days per week, that amounts to £1260 per year that you could have saved.

Always take a shopping list with you when you go to the shops, and only deviate from your list for something that you do need.

Time to stop justifying your spending

All of these justifications could be preceded by "Yes, but..." and there are many more beside this list, so if you have a "Yes, but" reason for your spending, you need to ask yourself critically what the basis is of your justification.

"I deserve a treat"

Everyone likes a treat every now and again and there is no reason why you shouldn't, but if you are buying treats for yourself every other day, that is nothing more than excessive indulgence. Buying things that will probably become next year's landfill whilst you have a large amount of debt is harmful to you in the long term. If your treats are mainly impulse buys, wait for a couple of days before buying something that you have seen to decide whether you really want it; you'll find in most cases that you don't. If you really can't do without it, you could also spend those couple of days looking online to see if it is cheaper elsewhere and save you money. Limit your treats in terms of expenditure and frequency, such as allowing yourself £20 per month; you can then set yourself a challenge to lessen that amount. If you reduce your monthly treats from £20 to £5, you will save £180 per year. Look for good items in charity shops and at car boot sales too – I once got a full bottle of Chanel Chance perfume for £2.

"I'm feeling down"

There are better ways to deal with low moods than buying something that will be languishing and forgotten in the back of a cupboard in a few months' time. It will give you a temporary rush of euphoria, but there is no substance to it and it won't last; the underlying problem will still be there. Exercise is best for lifting the spirits; go for a walk, go on a bike ride or have a swimming session. Alternatively you could also talk through how you feel with a friend or relative, as long as they are a person who uplifts you and won't make you feel even more depressed. Better still – do both at the same time and get someone to come with you on your walk, bike ride or swim. If you are feeling down a lot try the supplement St John's Wort, a GP once told me that it is a very good help for mild depression. If your depression is worse than mild, you must seek help from your GP as soon as possible.

"I can't help myself"

If your spending habits have become so obsessive that you truly cannot stop yourself, this has become an addiction that has an underlying psychological cause. The website of Addiction Helper describes shopping addiction:

"Shopping addiction, also known as compulsive shopping or omniomania, is probably the most socially acceptable – and socially reinforced – of the impulse control disorders. Shopping becomes a problem when it becomes out of control. The individual feels compelled to buy items they don't want and don't need, and they get a rush from the shopping experience. Despite efforts to stop their endless shopping, the shopaholic is unable to stop spending what is often money they do not have. There are usually underlying causes of an addiction to shopping; many addicts use shopping as a coping mechanism to deal with depression or intense emotions, such as anger or loneliness." [3]

---

[3] http://www.addictionhelper.com/addictions/shopping-addiction/

If you feel that this does not describe you, then you need to address your motivation in overspending, especially with impulse buys. Keep a diary of how you feel when you feel the need to overspend and look at ways in which you can deal with your feelings in a more positive way. Focus always on what are your wants and needs, and if you have spotted something that falls under the category of 'want', walk away and think about it for a few days.

"I buy things that save time and effort"

You may say this about buying a coffee before work instead of making your own, or for buying a sandwich for lunch. Be honest with yourself and ask yourself whether you could make time. When you get home, do you do a few chores for half an hour and then spend hours in front of the TV, or aimlessly surfing the net, or being social media's slave? Allot a bit of time to preparing some food for the next day. Do you really need expensive power tools and gadgets to save a few minutes? Having to put a bit of muscle into doing a job is good exercise for you and keeps you fit and healthy. I've never seen the point of a leaf blower, when a rake does the job just as well, is much cheaper to buy and doesn't use any fuel - which of course is an extra expense and an ongoing one too. You might miss the odd leaf, but will the sky cave in if there are a few leaves on the lawn?

"The Joneses have better things than me"

To hell with the Joneses; they are probably even more maxed out on their lines of credit than you are. If you have people around you who judge you on the things you have rather than your personality, it says everything about them and nothing about you. Trying to keep up with somebody else's extravagant lifestyle is a competition that nobody can ever win. There will always be someone who has more than you – if you have thousands, there are people with millions. If you have millions, there are people with billions. There are always new toys coming on the market as well, and once you have your spanking new toy that impresses everyone, a few months later there will be something better. Take a look at the news coverage of the queues of people who camp out overnight for the latest iPhone and who later walk out of the store clutching their new toy with glassy-eyed, hypnotic happiness; two updated versions of it come out every year.

I was once envious of a relative who always had the best; new cars, new furniture every couple of years, gorgeous clothes and fantastic holidays. The illusion broke one day when I was flicking through the Tjareborg brochure, the company through which she had just booked a holiday. Her young daughter pointed to a picture of the Tjareborg card (similar to a store card, used to buy holidays with extortionate interest if not paid off in full) and said, "Mummy's got one of those". Ha! I thought, as the bubble burst of the perfect lifestyle and I realised that she was probably deep in debt.

Some years later when the little girl had grown up I went to her hen party, a day at a health spa in a country house. She had grown up to be a sensible person, but I found the day excruciating as I found some of her friends to be insufferable. There was a core of 'queen bees' in their thirties and forties, and all they could talk about was clothes shopping, top spas they had visited and their fantastic holidays. I could see the envious expressions on the younger women who probably couldn't afford such luxuries, but it is this type of peer pressure that lures people into debt. I was still paying into the IVA at that point and it made me wonder whether they could truly afford that lifestyle. Thankfully I had brought a book with me and I managed to escape to a quiet part of the gardens for a good part of the day.

Another relative, highly materialistic and not a very nice person at all, also had the perfect spacious home, nice cars and holidays. She had left her bank statement lying on a table one day when I paid one of my duty visits (it was a duty, not a pleasure), and on just the uppermost page of the statement there were three £25 unauthorised overdraft charges.

"But everyone has debt – even the government"

As my mother used to say, "If all your friends decided to jump off a cliff, would you do so too?" If you think about it, this is a lemming approach to overspending and debt. You could say the same about other damaging behaviour – that you excessively smoke, binge drink, gamble or take recreational drugs because everyone else does around you. You do have free will and choices. It is also not true that everyone has debt. I have known several people who were extremely careful in managing their money, including one former colleague who always sneered at buying things 'on tick' and who never went abroad on holiday, always finding a reasonably priced caravan or cottage by the sea. He was a good-hearted person who enjoyed life without the need to spend recklessly. He had his mortgage paid off before he was 40, and that was with raising two children as well.

As for the government, I think that we all agree that we don't like politicians and they are a bunch of idiots. We're better than them, so let's start managing our money a lot more wisely than they do.

Bring your spending under control

Using credit can be a good thing if it is applied prudently and paid off as soon as possible so that it incurs less interest. You can use it for investments that will increase your assets and worth, such as:

- a mortgage
- a car or a season ticket to get you to work
- to pay for training to improve your job prospects

It is also helpful to tide you over an expensive short-term emergency, such as a big repair bill to your car or your home, provided that you get the bill paid off as quickly as possible so that you incur only a small amount of interest.

What it is not good for is a consumer binge on a ton of stuff that you don't need. Consider also that on most of the things you buy, 20% goes to the Treasury as VAT, so you're also increasing the amount of tax that you pay.

This step means that you need to end the use of your credit and store cards right now for any non-essential items. Leave all your cards at home (except a debit card if you do need something) when you go shopping. If you see a bargain, do you need it? Remember that if it's something that you would not have bought at the full price, you haven't saved anything. Use cash for small items.

Do you really need a brand new car? Its value depreciates the moment you drive it off the garage forecourt. In monetary terms cars are not assets that appreciate over time, unless you have a classic car that is sought after. There are plenty of cars on the market that are only about a year old, but you will save even more if you get a car that is four or five years old. There are plenty of comparison sites to help you look at a car's economy and reliability; an older car will perform just as well and not cost you as much in the first place.

Don't replace things that you already have if the things that you have already function properly. One of my friends was horrified that I use my 25-year-old Kitchen Devil knife for chopping veggies, as she wouldn't dream of using anything other than her top of the range chef quality knives and has threatened to get me a set. That's fine if it's a gift, but I'm not replacing my trusty old knife when it does the job so well.

If you need any new household goods, remember that trendy colours come with a larger price tag. I doubt if the manufacturers have to spend £50 more on red paint rather than white, you're simply paying more for a different look than white. I was looking online at stepladders the other day, the cheapest one (white colour) was £10 less than the others, but the dearer ones were trendy chrome. It's a stepladder for heaven's sake, not a fashion item – it's probably going to be in the shed for most of the time.

Set yourself a no-spend challenge

This is where you set yourself a strict limit on what you spend every day for a set period of time. Make it a long period of time though, so that it truly is a challenge. People who have done this say that it is very difficult at first, but once they are in the swing of the challenge they found it hard to spend money on things that they didn't need. Do an internet search for 'no spend challenge' and you will find a lot of advice and support; you could also persuade friends to join with you in the challenge, maybe as a way to save up for something specific such as holiday or Christmas expenses. It is a very good test of financial discipline, and it is far better to undertake this voluntarily than to be forced to do so, as I was when I entered into the IVA.

Team up with a money-saving buddy

If you know someone who is also struggling financially, team up with them to see how much money each of you can save. If you have a debt problem there is no need for your friend to know that if you don't want them to know about it; you could explain that you are trying to save money for something specific, such as Christmas or annual holiday expenses. Having support is a powerful motivator, like the motivation that people experience when they go to a slimming group where they find mutual support. Each of you can set a goal and you can compare your progress regularly.

Chapter Six

Planning your finances - and why many people don't

This would be a much better world if more married couples were as deeply in love as they are in debt.

- Earl Wilson

Just over half of Britain's households (56%) maintain a regular spending plan[1], so that means that nearly half don't do so. 'Winging it' is a sure-fire way of losing control of your money.

There are some reasons why you might not take the time to sit down and plan your spending. Some people have dyscalculia, also known as number dyslexia. Unfortunately this condition has been under-researched and under-resourced, but it is estimated that this condition is found amongst 3 to 6 percent of the population. People with dyscalculia have great difficulty in performing even the most basic arithmetic calculations. The British Dyslexia Association has information about dyscalculia on its website (www.bdadyslexia.org.uk), and dyscalculia researcher Dr. Anna J. Wilson has information on her website also (www.aboutdyscalculia.org).

---

[1] Money Advice Service press release, 26 December 2012

You may be under a lot of pressure with debt and possibly other pressures in your life; your money problems may be a burden shared with depression and other mental health problems. There is help available to help you to prepare a spending plan. There are many template plans online or if you would prefer someone to help you in person to prepare a budget, your local council may be able to provide you with details of organisations that might be able to help in your area.

If neither of those applies to you, it may be that you just have an aversion to maths; maybe, like me, you hated it at school. Budgeting however is arithmetic, not the full range of maths; there is no algebra, geometry, calculus or any of the rest of the complicated stuff. It is addition and subtraction in the main, and possibly some division and multiplication that can be done easily on a calculator – and you don't have to use any of those scientific function buttons. That's all that managing your spending entails – basic arithmetic. You don't need to understand how the global stock markets work or the intricacies of the country's government spending. Your fear becomes greater if you equate balancing your budget with the wider complexities of the financial world.

Maybe the scale of your spending is something that you don't want to face, but it is an essential step to take in order to start to take control of your finances. You cannot take control of a situation without knowing the facts. A recent report showed that a third of British young people aged 18 to 24 were too scared to check their bank account and they lose track of their spending[2]. I was in a similar position when I entered into the IVA. Though I had always kept a running balance of my bank account, when I added up our joint debts the total figure shocked me; I had never added up the total of what we owed, but I think that deep down I didn't want to know. You are not going to get a grip on the situation though if you don't know the figures.

Budgeting is compiling a list of all your monthly expenditures; rent/mortgage, Council Tax, utilities, food, transport costs and all other necessary expenditure. Don't forget expenditure that you might make once a year, such as insurance premiums and car tax; add those up and divide the total by 12. You then subtract your monthly expenditure from your monthly net salary and that is what you have left for your credit repayments.

It helps to create a spreadsheet for this but if you are not familiar with spreadsheets, a pen and paper version in a notebook will do. There are computer software and apps for managing your money that will provide visual graphics such as charts that show where your expenses go as it divides them up into categories. From the feedback I have seen an app that has become very popular is You Need A Budget, and users have stated that it has helped them enormously to reduce their debts and to start saving.

My personal view is that I am very wary of online and telephone banking and of software that links to your bank accounts. Hacking seems to be becoming increasingly sophisticated and I do not want to find

---

[2] http://www.thisismoney.co.uk/money/studentfinance/article-3442660/Third-young-adults-scared-check-bank-account.html

myself in the position of having my bank account emptied. It was a lot easier thirty years ago when most of my expenses were paid by cheque and I kept a running total of my balance (or, more often, the balance of my overdraft) in my cheque book. A man recently found that his bank balance had been emptied of his entire savings of about £22,700 by hackers who had hacked into his bank SMS messages by a practice known as 'smishing'[3]. You may feel that online banking and telephone banking is convenient, but you have to assess the convenience against the risk in having your accounts emptied. That could lead to a mortgage or rent payment not being made on time which would be classed as a payment in arrears, and having no funds available for food and other necessities whilst it is sorted out with your bank.

I also don't like the idea of the decline of cash as a payment, and some pundits are forecasting that cash will cease to exist in Britain in ten years' time. It is interesting that the decline in the use of cash is paralleled by a rise in debt in the UK and I have found it easier to keep my bank account in the black since I started to make most of my purchases in cash. Of course cash can be stolen, but so can your cards – as can the money in your bank account through a hacked electronic transfer. There is also a privacy issue should money cease to exist; every purchase you make will be logged and you don't know who will have access to that information. Finally, how would you buy things at car boot sales and through local ads, and will kids need bank accounts for their pocket money?

---

[3] http://www.thisismoney.co.uk/money/saving/article-3438512/Beware-smishing-scam-saw-one-Santander-customer-lose-23k.html

So from that digression my personal finance software of choice is one that I have loaded onto my PC that stands alone from any bank account. It provides graphs of my spending categories and provides me with a forecast of how much money I should have left at the end of the month. It also has a facility for multiple accounts. I have had the software for a few years now and it still serves me well.

There are also budget and debt planners available online, for example through the websites of The Money Advice Service and The Money Charity. You can find their contact details at the end of this book. Whatever method you use, ensure that you keep your accounts updated and monitor the progress of your spending regularly.

Chapter Seven

How to turn around your finances

It is hard to fail, but it is worse never to have tried to succeed.

- Theodore Roosevelt

Taking the first steps

There are three initial steps on the path to debt freedom:

- Admit that you have a problem
- Make a vow to yourself that you are going to resolve the problem
- List the total amount of what you owe

Above all, don't panic, especially after you have made a total of what you owe; you can escape from the misery of debt no matter how monumental the scale of it may seem and there is a lot of support out there to help you if you need it. Even if your debt repayments exceed your disposable income after you have budgeted for necessities, all is not lost; there is a solution.

Once you've done these steps, decide whether you feel strong enough to carry on alone or whether you need help, advice and support. There is no shame in asking for help; there is not one of us who can cope with every single thing at all points in our lives. The not-for-profit organisations that provide help with debt are trained at helping people with debt problems; they counsel many people with debt and they will not judge or blame you. Do be aware that there are some profit-making companies that on the surface seem to be debt help organisations. If you do an internet search for debt help, the not-for-profits usually have a website address with .org, and the commercial companies are .co.uk. If in doubt, click on their 'About us' page and see if they are a non-profit making organisation or not.

If you feel that you need support, find out if there is a support group near you. Debtors Anonymous has meetings at some locations in the UK and Ireland and they also hold Skype meetings. If they don't have a meeting near you, there are several independent meetings around the country. If an internet search doesn't come up with anything you might find through your GP surgery, local council or volunteer centre whether there is a local group, or you could phone or email debt advice organisations to ask if there is one near you. Churches also run debt support and counselling in some areas, I have heard that 'you don't have to be a believer and they don't try to convert you'.

Prioritise your debts

Priority debts are those that affect your home and basic needs:

- Mortgage or rent arrears
- Council tax

- Utilities, such as gas, electric and water

It is essential that any arrears with these be dealt with first, as you could lose your home and/or have your utilities cut off. Speak to your lender, landlord, council and utility companies to see what arrangement you can come to with them in order to get the arrears paid off. If you feel that you can't face talking to them, get help and support for this; useful organisations are listed at the end of this book. Do be aware though that you might find the lender, landlord, council etc more helpful than you think they might be; you won't be the first person they have spoken to with payment problems and going through legal processes to recover what they are owed costs them a lot of money.

Paying back in full versus in part

I have read a lot of comments that if you borrow money, you should pay it back in full rather than going along a route of paying part of it back and getting the rest written off, which is what can happen with an IVA. The argument for this is that it is a matter of honour; you entered into an agreement that you would repay what you owe, and I can see the logic in that. On the other hand financial institutions have acted less than honourably as we have seen in the PPI and mortgage endowment scandals and with excessive bank charges, not to mention their extortionate bonuses. The poor have also been fleeced through much higher interest rates, doorstep lending and payday loans through practices that are now widely considered to be unethical. Those are the two sides to the argument and I believe that you should weigh those up for yourself and follow your own rational thought and conscience.

If you owe money to an illegal money lender…

… also known as a loan shark; these are lenders who do not have permission from the Financial Conduct Authority to lend money. They rarely offer details of the loan in writing and borrowers often find that the loan of a small sum turns into a massive repayment. This situation can often turn vicious as they prey on the desperation of their victims who cannot borrow money from legitimate lenders and they enforce the repayments with threats and intimidation. The truth is that the loan is illegal and therefore you are under no obligation to repay an illegal loan, but there is no crime on your part in borrowing from them. The lenders may tell you that you could be prosecuted for borrowing with an illegal loan, but this is not true and you won't be prosecuted if you report them.

The Illegal Money Lending Team, based in Birmingham, has been set up by the National Trading Standards Board and investigates illegal moneylenders in the whole of England. You can contact them in confidence for advice, you can find their contact details are on their website at www.birmingham.gov.uk/stoploansharks. The National Trading Standards Board has set up similar teams in Scotland, Northern Ireland and Wales; contact details are at the back of this book. Do remember that loan sharks are growing rich on the misery of their victims so the more this despicable trade is wiped out, the better.

If you have borrowed from a payday or doorstep lender

The Financial Conduct Authority introduced new regulations for payday lenders in 2015 following an investigation of claims of irresponsible lending. It was alleged that the firms were lending sums that its customers could not afford and in some cases the interest rates were as high as 7000%. If you have had payday loans in the past, look into making a claim against the lender for unfair treatment for providing an unaffordable loan and you could get a refund which you can use towards paying off your debts. You will have a strong case if some of these apply:

- the lender did not make clear to you what fees or charges were payable;
- you had to 'roll over' the loan by consolidating it into a new loan;
- you had to borrow from another lender to pay the loan;
- the loan repayment was a large proportion of your income;
- the lender did not do credit checks.

Contact one of the debt help organisations listed at the back of this book for help and support with this. For a step-by-step guide to doing this yourself and template letters, read this article: www.debtcamel.co.ukpayday-loan-refunds/

If you are just about managing your repayments

Hopefully you are not yet at the point of a crisis where you cannot afford your repayments. If this is so, take it from me; you really don't want to reach the point of crisis as it is an awful place to be. If you can take action now to avoid reaching this point in the future, you will be better prepared to cope with any financial setbacks that you might face further down the line. Here are your steps:

- Draw up a budget.
- Stick to your budget.
- Stop shopping! Only buy things that you need and look critically at areas where you can save money. The chapters 'Revise your spending' and 'Money saving tips' will help you with this.
- Use most of your spare income towards paying more than your minimum repayment. There are two ways in which you can do this; either by concentrating on paying off first the smallest sum or the one with the highest interest rates, or to divide pro-rata between all the lenders with the higher payments going to lenders to whom you owe the most money. If a quick result of getting the smallest sum paid off sooner will give you more of a sense of achievement, go with that method.
- Use the rest of your spare income towards building an emergency fund and open a separate savings account to keep it in. Aim initially for a sum that will cover one month of your essential expenditure, and then carry on to increase this to three months' cover. This will help you to avoid using credit if you have a big unexpected and essential expense.
- Cut up your credit and store cards, though keep one credit card if you prefer for

emergencies *only* (or if you do need it, such as for car hire) until you have your contingency fund built up to a comfortable level. If you do keep one credit card, don't carry it with you unless you have an emergency expense.
- If you need to keep one credit card such as for car hire, ask for a reduced limit that only covers your essential expenditure and request that you have no further unsolicited limit increases.
- Sell stuff that you no longer want and use the cash towards the repayments to your lenders.
- Look at ways in which you can increase your income, such as getting seasonal or part-time work or self-employment. Check to see if there are any state benefits that you might be entitled to.
- Educate yourself in financial management, as it really is less complicated than it is made out to be.
- Once a credit or store card is paid off, cancel the account.

Your options if you can no longer afford your repayments

These are the basic outlines of the main options available to you (information correct as at June 2016). For further detailed information such as how your assets and your credit rating will be affected, have a look at various websites that offer help and advice such as Citizens Advice, StepChange or National Debtline. Conditions and criteria can differ, depending on where you live within the United Kingdom.

I would strongly advise you to speak to an advisor at one of the not-for-profit organisations listed at the back of this book, as each option has both benefits and risks depending on your circumstances. Everyone's circumstances vary, with variables such as income, level of debt, family circumstances and level of assets, and some options will be more appropriate for you than others. You can get an impartial assessment of your circumstances and the most appropriate solution for you by contacting one of the non-profit help organisations.

1. Make an agreement with your lenders yourself

This is an informal arrangement that you make directly with your creditors to pay them what you can afford from your disposable income. National Debtline has created a tool, CASHflow, that will help you to negotiate yourself with your creditors; you can find the details on their website.

The first thing that you need to do is to work out a budget of all your essential expenses, deduct this from your income and work out what you can repay per month. You should also ask them to consider freezing the interest so that the debt does not increase. You should expect to be treated fairly by your creditors, as you are offering them an option that will repay the debt in full in contrast to other options whereby part of the debt is written off, so it is in their interest to consider your proposal. If your proposal is turned down by any of your lenders or if they refuse to freeze the interest, seek advice from one of the charitable organisations, either by using the template letters on their websites or by contacting them by email or phone.

This option can take a long time to pay off, but it does have the advantage of being an informal arrangement and thus there are lesser risks to your home and employment than those that exist with other methods. Creditors could take court action against you, but attempts by a borrower to make an informal arrangement are recognised by courts. Make sure that you keep copies of all the letters that you send to your creditors and keep their replies.

2. Debt Management Plan (DMP)

This is an informal option that does not go through a court. You are eligible if you can afford a repayment of at least £5 per month and can pay off all your debts with your payment within 10 years. The plan must include all your creditors. Creditors are not obligated to freeze interest for the duration of a DMP, but if you enter a DMP your advisor may be able to persuade the creditors to freeze the interest. DMPs are flagged against your debts on credit reference agency reports.

You can arrange for the payment to be made by you to a debt management company, but these are profit-making companies that charge fees; Stepchange and National Debtline (both of which are charities) can set up a DMP free of charge. Do be aware that profit-making companies that arrange DMPs can become bankrupt, and I saw one newspaper report of this recently quoting one customer who had lost payments of about £10,000 made to her debt management company.

3. Debt Relief Order (DRO)

This is an option that does not go through a court and you are eligible if you live in England, Wales or Northern Ireland; Scotland has a similar scheme called a Minimal Assets Process bankruptcy, but the conditions vary.

To be eligible for a DRO you must meet the following basic criteria:

- Your unsecured debts must be less than £20,000 if you live in England and Wales, or less than £15,000 if you live in Northern Ireland;
- You do not own your home, either outright or mortgaged;
- Your assets are less than £1,000 in England and Wales, or less than £300 in Northern Ireland;
- You have less than £50 from your income after all your living costs are deducted.

There are certain criteria also regarding previous insolvencies and assets and also certain debts such as student loans cannot be included in a DRO. If you meet all the criteria you can apply for a DRO by paying a fee of £90 to the Insolvency Service. Your debts are then put on hold for 12 months and if your circumstances are still the same at the end of the 12 months, the debts are written off. Your name will also appear on the Individual Insolvency Register until 3 months after the DRO has ended.

4. Individual Voluntary Arrangement (IVA)

IVAs were set up as an alternative to bankruptcy and are administered on your behalf by an Insolvency Practitioner (IP). They are available for residents of England, Wales and Northern Ireland; there is a similar arrangement in Scotland called a Protected Trust Deed. National Debtline and Stepchange can help you to get in touch with an IP recommended by them.

The normal criteria to be eligible for an IVA are:

- you have at least 3 debts, the total of which is at least £10,000;
- your debts are owed to at least two different lenders;
- you have at least £100 spare income after essential expenditure per month;
- you can pay into the IVA at least 10p for each £1 that you owe.

Certain debts are excluded, such as student loans. If a certain proportion of your creditors agree to the proposal of the IVA it will be registered at a court. Some IPs will require a fee up front but others deduct the fee from your monthly repayments. The term of the IVA is normally 5 years and any debts still outstanding at the end of the IVA are written off. Details of the IVA will be recorded with credit reference agencies for the duration of the IVA, and then for one year after it has ended.

There are certain conditions relating to home ownership and assets that you should look into carefully before entering into an IVA. If you are able to access pension funds, for example if you are allowed to access them when you reach the age of 50 or 55 and you have reached this age or will do so during the period of the IVA, this could jeopardise your pension. Entering into an IVA can also have adverse consequences for certain types of employment.

Your name will also appear on the Individual Insolvency Register until 3 months after the IVA has ended. The IVA will be noted with credit reference agencies during the IVA and for one year after its completion.

5. Bankruptcy

Bankruptcy is an option that needs to be considered very carefully; this is a brief outline and you should look into it further as there are many more conditions that may mean that it is unsuitable for you. This is an option that goes through a court (though you do not need to attend the court), and if you decide to make yourself bankrupt you must start the application online. A creditor can also apply for a debtor to be declared bankrupt. The current fee that you will have to pay to do this is £655, which can be paid by instalments. If your application is approved, you will be appointed an Official Receiver who will examine your assets and income. The bankruptcy order normally ends after one year but your spare income, after taking into account your essential expenses, will be paid to the Official Receiver for three years.

Any valuable assets that you own will be sold to pay your creditors, though your car might be exempt if you require it for work or family reasons and any items such as tools that you need for work are exempt. If you are able to access pension funds, for example if you are allowed to access them when you reach the age of 50 or 55, and you have reached this age or will do so during the period of bankruptcy, this could jeopardise your pension. There are certain stipulations for homeowners, so if you own your home you should look into this carefully.

Bankruptcy can affect your employment and could bar you from any professional bodies that you belong to. The bankruptcy order will be registered with credit reference agencies for six years after its commencement date. Your name will also appear on the Individual Insolvency Register until 3 months after the bankruptcy has ended.

Chapter Eight

Money-saving tips

Watch the pennies and the pounds will look after themselves.

- English saying

Some of my personal money-saving tips

You can find many tips to save money in books and online, and many are the same ones repeated though you do come across some innovative ones in every list. That's not a bad thing though to have the same message repeated so that it sticks in your mind. A simple way to access them online is to search for 'money saving tips' (adding 'UK' if you want the results to be specific to Britain; add here the country of your choice) and you will come across a lot of ideas that will help you to save money.

These are some of my own, or common ones with my own perspective.

- If you want to eat out and there is a further education college near you, find out if they offer courses in catering. If they do, the catering department might have a restaurant, staffed by its students, that offers meals to the public at a fraction of the cost that you would pay elsewhere. My mum often used to take me for a three-course lunch at our local FE college and the food and service were superb.

- Similarly, if the college also does courses in hairdressing and beauty, the department will probably have a salon that offers hairdressing and beauty therapy at a fraction of the high street cost. I have found that it does take longer for the students to cut hair and they have their work checked by their tutors, but allow time for this and have some patience – they are learning and this is invaluable experience for them.
- Do you really need to have your hair done at an expensive high street salon? Don't dismiss hairdressers who work from home, some of them do so because they need to have flexibility for family commitments. I go to my hairdresser's home where she has created a small salon, she used to work as a senior stylist at a top salon and I get a top of the range haircut at a fraction of the price.
- Skip the £2 coffee on your way to work and the £3 bought sandwich for lunch – make your own to take with you. I have a Thermos mug for taking coffee with me on the way to work, and I make my own sandwiches and snacks for lunch with tomatoes and fruit. That will save you about £1,200 per year. I also cook at the weekend a batch of snacks to take to work, such as fruit bars or flapjacks. If you spend 70p on a chocolate bar each day instead, that would cost about £200 per year.
- If you feel that you can't cook, consider learning; it's a skill, not a talent, and skills can be learned. It's also a life skill. See if there are

local classes or if that's out of your budget, find a friend who is willing to teach you the basics or look for 'how to cook' videos online.

- To save time, cook meals in bulk that can be frozen in batches, such as pasta sauces, curries and casseroles. It will also save money on fuel costs whilst cooking. My basic tomato pasta sauce is in an appendix towards the end of this chapter. I learned the recipe from an Italian, everyone who has had it has complimented it and it's very cheap and easy to make.

- Once you've opened a jar of curry paste, it will soon go off if you don't use up the rest. When the jar is opened, freeze the rest by open freezing it in tablespoon-size portions on a baking tray, and once it's frozen keep it in a closed container in the freezer.

- Food that is ruined through overcooking is money wasted, so if you're prone to forget something on the hob or in the oven, set an alarm for the end time.

- Buy your fruit, veg and salad from a market if you can, it is often more fresh and cheaper.

- If you feel that you must have a holiday, consider house sitting and pet sitting for a low-cost holiday. Several sites match up homeowners and sitters for a modest fee and there are properties not only in the UK but also abroad.

- Allocate some time to entering free-to-enter competitions, though I would suggest that you set up a separate email account for this purpose as you will get a lot of marketing emails (don't let them tempt you to spend!).

It's time-consuming and you won't be lucky with a lot of them, but there's no cost to you other than your time. I entered a lot of competitions without getting anywhere, but then out of the blue I had an email to tell me that I'd won a ferry crossing and a short break in France. Check your competition email account regularly – I almost missed out on the France break because when I saw the email, I only had three days left to claim it.

- Grow some food. You don't need to be an expert gardener; I find that onions, strawberries and tomatoes are particularly easy to grow and the taste that strawberries and tomatoes have when freshly picked is wonderful. The basics of gardening aren't rocket science; they are easy to learn. If you don't have a suitable plot of land that you can dig up, many things can be grown in containers.
- If your water consumption is metered, install a water barrel to collect rainwater for your garden. Using tap water for your garden will increase your water bill.
- If you are economical with your water usage in your home and pay a fixed water rate charge, consider having a water meter installed. I paid about £33 per month for fixed water rates until I moved into a house with a water meter; my monthly payment dropped to £12. Putting a brick in your water cistern saves water usage; it has no effect on the efficiency of the flush and uses about a litre less of water.
- Have a declutter and sell things that you no longer want or need on eBay, Amazon, Gumtree or at car boot sales. Other places to

advertise your unwanted stuff include notice boards at your workplace, corner shops, supermarkets and there may be a local community website where you can advertise. If your community website doesn't have a classifieds page for local people, contact the website to suggest it. Donate the rest that is difficult to sell to a charity shop rather than throwing it out.

- If you know a type of product well, look to see if you can buy it cheaply at car boot sales in order to sell on. A friend of mine looks out for designer label clothing that she then sells on eBay and she very rarely buys full price clothing for herself any more.

- If there's a skill that you want to learn or if you want to find out how to do one specific thing, search YouTube. You can find tutorials there on how to do pretty much everything and there are many videos on how to repair things. As a friend of ours said, "YouTube is the Haynes manual for everything".

- 'Buy cheap, buy twice', goes the old saying. If you need to buy something, save up in order to lay out a bit more expense (not using credit of course) to buy something of a fairly good quality that will last, especially if it is something that you are going to use a lot. I bought Le Creuset pans 27 years ago and they're still going strong today. I don't feel the need to buy new pans and I don't care if there are now more trendy colours – why should I, when my old ones are lasting so well?

- If you have an ebook reader, do an Amazon search for 'Kindle free books'. There are quite a few duds but also some hidden gems. Some writers offer their new books for free for a limited time promotion.

- Use your library to borrow books and rent DVDs. Many libraries now have an online system for reserving books for that bestseller that is coming out soon. You can also research your family history for free as libraries have free access to genealogy subscription sites, which will save you costly subscriptions.
- Arrange a 'present pact' for Christmas and birthdays with your family and friends, especially if you feel that they are feeling the pinch too. This is to decide that you will agree on a spending limit for presents, or to buy presents only for the children in the family. If they ask why, tell them that you are trying to save money – all the other details behind that are your business alone.
- Allot some time to read the personal finance columns of newspapers, either in print or online. You may not understand it all or find it interesting to start with, but it does sink in and will help you to become more knowledgeable about managing your finances. You will also come across articles that will help you to save money.
- Check out the notice board of your local library for free and low cost events.
- Get together with friends and colleagues with similar interests to share the cost of monthly magazines that you can pass around each other.

Investing in your health – a long-term saving

You may be in your 20s, 30s or 40s and still feel fit and strong and thoughts of old age and infirmity may be far from your thoughts. It is possible to remain fit and strong from your 50s onwards (barring accidents and serious health problems) by investing in your health now. From my first-hand knowledge of friends and family who have had the misfortune to have unexpected and serious health problems, I am fully aware of the extra financial costs that ill health can incur and of the ensuing worry and anxiety. With spending cuts, it is looking increasingly likely that you will not be able to expect the state services to solve in an instant any mobility problems that you might have in later life. Any bad habits like overeating, smoking, lack of exercise, recreational drug use or excessive drinking that harm your health may not be manifesting in problems now, but they will be storing up to blindside you at some point in the future.

There is no secret or magical elixir to maintaining your weight. Food is fuel – it's as simple as that. Think of your body as if it were your car; if you put the wrong fuel into your car, you will have a car that's not going anywhere. If your diet is mainly processed food, fat, sugar, chemicals and carbohydrates, your body isn't getting the essential nutrients it needs. I know so many people who follow faddish diets and their weight goes up and down like a yoyo. You also eat more if your diet consists of mainly processed food as you are not getting enough nutrients. Maintaining a healthy diet that provides you with essential nutrients and combining that with regular exercise is the best way to lose weight and stay healthy for the rest of your life. It also strengthens your immune system, which puts your body in a stronger position to fight disease. A good diet is another area of life that requires moderation and discipline rather than overindulgence. It is often said that nothing is bad for you in moderation and I do believe that, but it seems to be the case with a lot of people that they forget the word 'moderation' is in that saying. I do like sweet things (I am particularly partial to Swiss and Belgian chocolate) but I eat them moderately and I have a diet that has plenty of wholefoods, fruit, vegetables and salad.

Only do exercise that you enjoy. I went to a gym once and vowed never to visit one again; I think that they look like torture chambers and they cost a fortune. That's my view though, carry on with the gym if you enjoy it. My preferred exercise is walking – it's free apart from the outlay of sturdy boots and a windproof jacket (both of which last for years) and you get to see a lot when you are travelling at a slower pace. Do find a companion to go with you if you feel concerned for your safety when walking on your own or join a ramblers' group. Make the effort to walk somewhere if it is less than a mile rather than taking the car. You probably walk a lot if you have a dog, but if you don't and you like dogs, do you have a friend or neighbour who might appreciate some dog walking help, especially if they are elderly? If you live or work in a building with a lift, take the stairs instead – if that really is too much, stop the lift one floor below and walk up one flight.

Other inexpensive ways to exercise are swimming and cycling. Swimming baths offer discounts if you go regularly and they sometimes hold fitness classes too. Cycling requires the outlay of a bicycle (you could find one secondhand) and a helmet; buy the helmet new though, as you won't know if a secondhand one has had an impact.

To follow an exercise programme such as yoga or Pilates, have a look at YouTube to see if there is a video that you can follow; you could rope in some friends if you have the space in your front room and make it a regular meet-up. You might also find a suitable exercise DVD or video in a charity shop – some people try them for a while and then lose interest. If you have satellite or cable channels, you can find fitness programmes on there too.

Take care of your back, as back problems can be debilitating. Do stretches regularly through the day if you sit all day at a computer and always bend your knees instead of bending down from your lower back, especially if you are lifting something.

Cooking

I have heard people say smugly that they can't cook, as if it's a badge of honour. I have heard some women say that cooking is 'slavery for women', but I believe that women should learn to cook – and so should men. *Everyone* should learn to cook; it's a life skill. I was horrified to hear from an 18-year-old undergraduate that her lessons in cookery at school consisted of a lot of theory and then they made things from packets. Fortunately a relative had taught her to cook. If it is the case that young people are not learning the basics either from their parents or at school, then cooking will become a dying skill. I sometimes wonder how the nation would cope if wartime conditions ever returned with the introduction of rationing and imports severely restricted; far more of our food is now imported as a lot of farmland has now been sold for housing and it would be highly unlikely that you would get your current range of ready meals. There are now 20 million more people to feed in the UK than in 1945. I know that sounds rather pessimistic and depressing, but we have become complacent in a prolonged time of peace in Europe and consider war to be distant both in time and place. I remember my grandmother telling me that she told off my grandfather for joining the armed forces Reserves as there might be another war. "Don't be daft, there won't be another war", he said. That conversation took place in July 1939.

I am glad that I learned cookery and sewing at school, though I would have liked also to have learned woodwork but that was only for boys in the 1970s. Although I'm not a brilliant cook I'm not a bad one either; I know the basics of cooking and I can make almost anything. I have a well-thumbed copy of the Reader's Digest classic cookbook *The Cookery Year* that has an excellent and comprehensive reference section on all the basic skills. I still have the skills to do dressmaking occasionally and I can repair my clothes to make them last.

You should really ask yourself if you are going to use the latest cookery gadget on the market or whether it will be money down the drain. How many yoghurt makers, panini presses and chocolate fountains languish and gather dust in the recesses of Britain's cupboards? Do people really buy rice cookers – what's wrong with a pan? I read that a gadget is going to be on sale soon for £90 that will butter bread in three seconds. Come on, it really isn't that arduous and it doesn't take forever to make a sandwich, but I guess that for some people it's a couple of precious minutes away from Facebook.

Some gadgets are worthwhile investments if you are going to use them often. I still have my mother's Kenwood Chef that I remember from early childhood, still going strong today, and my other two essentials are my blade processor and hand blender, but that is about the limit of my gadgets. Another good gadget investment has been my bread maker. I couldn't get on with the bread maker when I first bought it but I was using recipes from the manufacturer's handbook. I then bought *Bread Machine Baking* by Jennie Shapter for £2 in a charity shop; I used those recipes and have never looked back. One tip on bread machine baking – if you boil potatoes, save the water from the pan for bread making, it makes a much moister loaf. Use the water within a day or it will go off. I make an organic granary loaf with high quality flour for about 60p that lasts me a week and the savings I have made on bread have paid for the cost of the bread maker many times over. If you are going to say that I could have saved money by buying 15p loaves of sliced bread from value ranges, remember what I said before about food as fuel. I economise as much as I can on food shopping, but I won't eat poor quality food as it's not good for you. Mass-produced loaves aren't baked properly anyway – look up the Chorleywood bread process. I also despair at the quality of a lot of fruit and veg on sale in Britain, as in comparison to the quality you find across the Channel it is mainly rubbish. Many Britons don't seem to understand food like other Europeans; it is impossible to sell poor quality food in nations like France, Spain or Italy as their customers simply wouldn't buy it.

Some things are very easy to make, cost much less than shop-bought and take little time. One thing that I never buy is coleslaw as it is only shredded cabbage, grated carrot and finely chopped onion that you put in a bowl and mix with mayonnaise. It's really quick and easy to make. Cheap supermarket coleslaw tastes like sour mush to me; homemade tastes like the expensive coleslaw that you find in upmarket 'deli' ranges and is a fraction of the price. You can also vary it by using red cabbage instead of white, or by replacing onion with spring onions or shallots.

Do you really need to buy a bag of chopped veg or salad, or grated cheese? It really doesn't take much time and effort to chop those up or to grate cheese and it is much cheaper to buy them whole for you to chop or grate yourself. Finally, you always know what goes into food that you prepare yourself; there's never any horsemeat in a lasagne that I make.

Fashion

Are you truly an individual if you follow the fashion herd? What does that say about your autonomy as a human being if a handful of people are telling you what to wear?

It matters a lot to teenagers when social bonding and acceptance is important but then you grow up and become more settled in your own identity, so why does fashion matter? I came to a stage a few years ago where I didn't care what I wore was fashionable or not, I would buy clothes that don't date and I still wear clothes that I have had for many years. I have spent less than £200 on clothes in the past five years, and that includes my charity shop finds. Two years ago I went to a wedding and wore a dress that I had bought twenty years previously; it was a classic style and the colours were gorgeous. Several people commented on how pretty it was and there wasn't a single comment along the lines of "OMG, that is sooo 90s!!!".

If you care about the environment, consider the pollution that arises from the fashion trade. A huge amount of pesticides are used on cotton, 60% of which is used for clothing. The clothes manufacturing trade in Britain is now a pale shade of what it used to be, as retailers sought to be more competitive and outsourced clothing manufacture abroad where wages are low and many workers (mainly women) lost their jobs as clothing factories closed. I remember a time when Marks and Spencer used to say that all its goods were manufactured in Britain; this is no longer the case. Allegations of clothes manufacturers' use of child labour in developing world countries continue to surface regularly. There is a far higher carbon footprint with having most of Britain's clothes imported from the other side of the globe, as this requires them to be sent in cargo ships that use massive amounts of fuel for the journey.

My advice is; buy classic clothes that don't date. Examine your motivation if you are buying an excessive amount of clothes. Recycle clothes that you no longer need by taking them to a charity shop or selling them online or at a car boot sale rather than throwing them away. Look for bargains at charity shops and car boot sales, you will be surprised how many show little or no sign of wear and sometimes they still have the tags on.

DIY

I came across a newspaper article that I found hilarious, but it was also saddening. It related how Britain's DIY skills are on the decline and how a survey of men found that:

- Only one in five can mend a leaking tap;
- Less than half can wire a plug;
- Three out of five would call a plumber to unblock a toilet.[1]

I can do two of those and my husband can do all three; I would leave the leaky tap to him. He is good at basic plumbing, electrics and generally fixing broken things and I am fairly good at painting and can hang wallpaper very well; I learned from watching my father doing the decorating. When you consider that a call-out fee might be about £50, it seems that a lot of people are paying through the nose for jobs that are really easy to do. Whilst this was a survey of men I see no reason why women should not also learn some basic DIY. I did find this survey shocking, as I remember from my childhood that almost all men did a lot of DIY jobs and also did basic maintenance on their cars. Why have these skills not been passed on?

You do need to know your limits though; I would never consider knocking down an internal wall, as I wouldn't know whether it might be a retaining wall. Knock one of those down and your house will probably collapse. Never, never do anything with a

---

[1] www.telegraph.co.uk/men/thinking-man/practically-incompetent-how-britain-gave-up-on-diy/

gas system or appliance unless you are a Gas Safe registered engineer, only tackle electrical work if you are completely confident that you know what you are doing and know your limits with plumbing as a leak can cause serious structural damage. You can learn the basics though from a good manual or from learning from someone who is proficient in DIY. B&Q also run reasonably priced courses at some of their stores.

Some basic car maintenance knowledge can also save you money. We had a clapped-out radiator in our car whilst on an IVA-induced budget, and when I looked in the Haynes manual in the library I found that changing the radiator is classed as being in the 'easy' skills set. All that it required was to unclip some hoses and unscrew some nuts and bolts, put in the radiator and then reconnect everything up. We got a brand new radiator for about £60 and changed it ourselves. We have had no problems with it since.

Basic tomato pasta sauce
Ingredients
1 tablespoon of olive oil
1 medium onion
Half a teaspoon each of dried basil, oregano and marjoram
1 tin chopped tomatoes
1 teaspoon of tomato puree
Salt and pepper

Method
Add olive oil to a heavy-based pan and warm under a low heat.
Finely chop the onion and add to the oil and add the dried herbs.

Stir until the onion is transparent and not browned, and then add the tinned tomatoes and puree.

Bring almost to the boil and then turn down to a very low heat, leave to simmer for about an hour until the liquid has reduced by about a third.

Add salt and pepper to taste.

This freezes well; double, triple or quadruple the quantities to make batches for the freezer.

The long cooking time reduces the liquid in the sauce and brings out the rich flavour of the tomatoes.

Use Italian Mixed Herbs if you like, but I never do; it's something that you would never find in a supermarket or alimentare in Italy. Italians mix together herbs themselves.

This is a basic sauce, so you can tinker about with the ingredients and add things like garlic, peppers or capers.

If you add some ground chilli peppers just before adding the tomatoes, this will make an arrabbiata sauce.

Always add salt and pepper near the end of the cooking time when cooking on the hob; if you add them at the start, it impairs the flavour.

Epilogue

Debt is normal. Be weird.

- Dave Ramsey

The process of writing has given me the opportunity to look back and reflect on my life's journey and to see clearly the painful truth of the havoc that debt has caused in my life. I could weep when I consider how much we paid in mortgage payments and credit interest and now we have so little to show for it. It is evident to me now that I did not focus on long-term security, I just focused on the present moment and could not see the consequences until everything fell apart. I now see clearly that in the early years, spending was a way to bolster my low self-esteem and made me feel more powerful - but as the years went on and I felt more at ease with myself, my overspending had become an ingrained habit. The truth is though that buying things didn't make me feel better about myself; what did make me feel more comfortable with myself was the process of overcoming my introversion, engaging with people and building strong friendships. It was easy to be reckless when I was in my 20s, 30s and 40s at a time when I felt strong and invincible, but now I am in my early 50s and I realised that I was facing an old age of poverty. Fortunately I had paid into a Civil Service pension scheme for a long time, but I could foresee that being swallowed up with paying housing rent that is rising all the time and having very little left over for basic living expenses. Longevity seems to run on both sides of my family (even my chain-smoking grandfather lived to 80), so if genetics do play a part in longevity I don't want to have an extended old age in abject poverty.

Now that I am debt-free (apart from my student loan mentioned before, due to be paid off very soon), I am able to focus on the next decade and a bit with a view to building a secure future. I keep an eye on global affairs and finance news and I see a global situation with a great deal of uncertainty, so I am shortly to start retraining in accountancy which is widely considered to be a recession-proof occupation. I have a plan for me and my husband to own a home outright by the time we both reach state pension age. This will entail sacrifices; as much as I would love to go to Canada to visit my cousin, our security has to come first. We have had some wonderful holidays in Britain over the years, so any holidays will be close to home.

Maybe I have my grandfather's determination to get back up again after falling. I wasn't the first in my family to have faced bankruptcy, as my grandfather became bankrupt in the 1930s. He came from a poor background but was good at mechanics; he repaired machines in factories and then went on to own a factory. After bankruptcy he rebuilt his fortunes and owned several factories after the war; when he died his estate was worth just over £25,000, which is the equivalent of about £500,000 in today's value. Yes, I made stupid choices in the past, but I am not going to compound that stupidity by continuing to make poor financial choices. Living prudently is the sensible path – and the only path - for me to take.

Above all, I am never going back to a life of debt. My money mismanagement ended in spectacular failure, but the real failure is not to learn from your mistakes. Making that first step to ask for help was the biggest and hardest step, but it brings you a wealth of benefits and well-being. Being forced into an IVA taught me the discipline that I needed and gave me a radical rethinking of spending, and my life has improved considerably for going through this experience. It also led me to think more deeply and critically about the reasons why debt has become such a plague of modern life. I no longer have the sinking feeling of seeing credit card bills on the mat or of checking the state of my overdraft. It is thrilling to have a bank account in the black and to have savings. I take pride in how I adapted to living within my means and the inventive ways and habits that I adopted in order to do this. I rarely buy anything new now, and I was delighted after finding a £5 secondhand pair of what looked to be high quality trousers with no signs of wear, to find out later that the brand retails at about £100. I was also put off prudent money management in the past by thinking that it was complicated, but when I started to make an effort to educate myself about financial matters I realised that they were simpler than I thought.

I have come to appreciate that a rich life is not about material things. My life is rich because of the wonderful people in my life, my happy marriage that has lasted for many years, the beauty of nature, my good health and the wisdom that I have gained from my life experiences and from reading widely. These have far greater importance to me than any of my material possessions and have brought me a greater sense of happiness, peace and contentment. My life is not all plain sailing; I have problems to deal with from time to time, but not having the additional problem of debt to worry about puts me in a far stronger position to cope with whatever comes my way. I heard a saying a while ago, 'The best things in life aren't things' and I agree with that completely. Happiness is not a life without troubles or worry; it is a state of mind despite the troubles and worry. Even through the IVA I had happy times; days out, watching good movies, meeting up with friends. I did worry throughout the IVA that another catastrophe could make the IVA fail and veer us into bankruptcy, but I worried unnecessarily as that didn't happen and getting out of debt misery was a far more positive thought. When I look back on my life and at the biggest problems that I have faced, I realise that overcoming them made me much stronger and wiser as a result. Meeting my problems head-on got easier with practice; I became a victor and a survivor, rather than a victim, through my triumphs.

Consumerism and living beyond one's means through overspending on stuff that you don't need is largely seen to be normal now. Perfectly good and usable things are discarded when a different colour or design becomes the latest trend. It has become socially acceptable to satisfy your every desire instantly, whether it may be a pair of designer shoes, an exotic holiday or a flashy new car, and it seems to me that this comes not only from peer pressure but also the media egg this on. I desired luxury items when I was young but I am now older, much wiser and, as I would like to think, more sensible. I would like to see prudence, thrift, responsibility, saving and living within our means as the new cool way of living.

People would be much happier if this should ever come to pass.

Perhaps you could write down your own story and reflect on the motivation and reasoning behind your spending that has led to debt. It will enable to you make connections and to see the trigger points that made what was possibly a bad situation worse. Be honest with yourself, even if seeing it in black and white shocks you and keep it private if it is intensely personal. Look at your emotional triggers that have led you to overspend and try to get into the habit of using logical and rational thinking in the choices that you make, rather than being at the mercy of your emotions. Do get help and support; there are several organisations listed at the end of this book that can help you on your journey out of debt. Remember the golden rule for shopping at all times – do you need it? Above all, make the decision to become debt-free – you will never regret it. Good luck, and I wish you wealth, health, happiness and peace.

Useful organisations

Warning! If you do an online search for 'debt help', some of the results will be profit-making companies who will benefit from advising you to enter into bankruptcy or an IVA. Their web address often includes co.uk. The following are not-for-profit organisations apart from one, where stated. The following information is correct at June 2016.
Some websites have a link to advice relating specifically to Scotland, Wales or Northern Ireland – these are usually shown at the top of the web page.

The Money Charity
www.themoneycharity.org
Education, information and advice on money matters, policy shaping, runs money management workshops.

National Debtline
www.nationaldebtline.org
Debt helpline - 0808 808 4000
Advice and information on debt. They also administer Debt Management Plans free of charge and can recommend an IVA practitioner from their panel.

StepChange
www.stepchange.org
Helpline - 0800 138 1111
Information and advice on debt, budgeting and money awareness. They also administer Debt Management Plans free of charge. Their subsidiary (a registered charity) can also administer IVAs. They have dedicated pages of information for each country

within the UK and they also have a website and helpline for the Republic of Ireland:
http://www.stepchangedebtcharity.ie
Helpline for Republic of Ireland -1800 937 435

Citizens Advice
www.citizensadvice.org.uk
Helpline for England - 03444 111 444 (see website for further contact options)
Advice service on a broad range of legal and consumer issues, including debt advice. Campaigns on citizen rights.

Debt Camel
www.debtcamel.co.uk
A very user-friendly website on debt advice that was set up by a Citizen's Advice Bureau advisor. It has a good section to help you decide on which method of debt solution is best for you.

Addiction Helper
www.addictionhelper.com
Helpline - 0800 915 9400 (24 hour service)
Help and advice for addictions, including shopping addiction. This is run by a company, not a non-profit organisation, but their website states that they give impartial advice including information about free resources such as the NHS.

Church Action on Poverty
www.church-poverty.org.uk
National campaigning on poverty issues including debt, they also run local support groups and projects throughout the country.

Debtors Anonymous UK
debtorsanonymous.org.uk
Organiser of debtor support groups including phone and Skype meetings, also offers lone support for people who are not near a meeting.

Christians against Poverty
https://capuk.org
Local support and counselling for help with debt and addictions; they run job search and money courses.

Loan Shark Teams
https://www.gov.uk/report-loan-shark
England: Helpline – 0300 555 2222
Wales: Helpline – 0300 123 3311
Scotland: Helpline – 0800 074 0878
Northern Ireland: Helpline – 0300 123 6262

Turn2us
www.turn2us.org.uk
Provides advice and help for people in financial need.

Recommended reading and viewing

These are books and films that I have found particularly educational; check to see if the books are in your local library and whether the films are on Youtube.

Books

How to Get Out of Debt, Stay Out of Debt and Live Prosperously: Mundis, Jerrold; Bantam, revised edition 2004
This is an excellent book based on the support programme Back to the Black which started in the USA. It goes into depth about the emotional and psychological issues surrounding debt and the resistance to facing the problem as well as providing a great deal of practical advice for many different types of personal circumstances. It provides a very detailed 'how to' section on approaching creditors yourself.

Britain's Personal Debt Crisis: Gibbons, Damon; Searching Finance Ltd., 2014
An excellent and thorough overview of the historical beginnings of the debt explosion and its effects on British society.

The Truth in Money: Thoren, Theodore R. & Warner, Richard F.; revised edition 1994
This is now out of print but can be found secondhand. It provides an accessible and easy to understand explanation of banking and credit, including an

explanation of why there will never be enough money in the world to pay off all outstanding debt.

Influence: The Psychology of Persuasion: Cialdini, Robert B.; Harper Business, revised edition 2007
Written by a psychology professor, it outlines how people can use psychology to make you do what they want. Be warned that it has been highly rated by sales and marketing professionals so that they can use it against their customers in order to make a sale; read this and you will recognise their tactics.

Art of Money Getting, or, Golden Rules for Making Money: Barnum, P.T.; Wilder Publications 2011
Although this was written in 1880, it is a wonderfully timeless read by one of America's most famous showmen. Barnum wrote with simplicity and common sense on the principles of financial prudence and his advice is still relevant today. As its copyright has now expired, this is available as a free creative commons ebook on Amazon (information correct as at May 2016).

Films

Starsuckers: Atkins, Chris; 2009
Great insight into how so many people become hooked on celebrity cuture and how celebrity publicity is artificial.

The Century of the Self: Curtis, Richard; 2002
An excellent account of the rise in tandem of advertising, consumerism and individualism in the 20th century.

Four Horsemen: Ashcroft, Ross; 2012
This is a very accessible overview of the faults in the global finance system and how this plagues the world today, benefitting the rich and impoverishing the rest.

Websites

Do bear in mind with the forums listed here that not all the replies will be by people who are qualified practitioners in the areas concerned. They are useful for guidance, but you should double-check any advice that you receive. This isn't a huge list, as I prefer not to spend most of my life online.

www.thisismoney.co.uk
A very accessible financial news website with a lot of subsections and guides on personal finance.

www.petrolprices.com
Useful tool for checking for the cheapest car fuel in your area, they have also started the Big Energy Switch to help its members to switch to the cheapest energy providers.

www.iva.co.uk
Help and advice pages and forum for people in an IVA, well worth a look before you consider entering into an IVA.

www.diseasecalleddebt.com
This is an excellent blog by Hayley, she and her husband cleared £41,000 of debt.

www.consumeractiongroup.co.uk
Advice forum on consumer issues. Their email newsletter is usually very informative.

www.mysupermarket.co.uk
Comparison site for supermarket prices.

www.futurelearn.com
Learn something new for free! Futurelearn has a wide range of free short courses delivered via the internet. They are currently running courses on numeracy and money management.

www.daveramsey.com
The website of American finance expert Dave Ramsey. The site has an American emphasis and Britons may find his style rather evangelical, but it has some interesting information and advice; there are plenty of articles.

Index

Advertising 36-41
Author's IVA 17-22, 66, 72, 106, 107
B&Q courses 102
Bagdikan, Ben 40
Banking 28-30
Bankruptcy 86
Basic needs 59
Bernays, Edward 38
Bieber, Justin 49
British Dyslexia Association 70
Budget planners 72
Budget software 72
Budgeting 70-74
Buy to Let 26
Car boot sales 91
CASHflow 82
Celebrity culture 43-51
Chelsea Girl 46
Christianity 33, 51
Church Action on Poverty 33
Cinema 42
Citizens Advice 19, 81
Community Links 33
Competitions 90
Cooking 89, 90, 96-99
Curtis, Adam 38
De Niro, Robert 45
Debt Management Plan 83

Debt Relief Order 84
Debtors Anonymous 76
Depression 1, 62, 63, 71
Diana, Princess of Wales 44
DIY 101, 102
Doorstep lender 79
Dunbar, Professor Robin 50
Dyscalculia 70
eBay 46, 91
Essential expenditure 72
Exercise 58, 59, 95, 96
Facebook 47
Fashion 99, 100
Finance news 93
Financial Conduct Authority 79
Focus group 39
Fractional reserve 29
Freud, Sigmund 38
Gardening 91
Gucci 46
Hacking 72
Hairdressing 89
Hanson, Lord 31
Health 94-96
Holidays 90
Homelessness 32
Housing 26-28

Illegal Money Lending Team 78
Illusory reality 55
Impulse buys 61
Individual Voluntary Arrangement (IVA) 85, 86
Inner child 56, 57
iPhone 65
Italy 27
Jackson, Michael 47
Kidulthood 56, 57
Kindle 92
King, Stephen 45
Leibovitz, Annie 47
Library 93
Loan shark 78
Longford, Lord, 48
Lucas, George 45
Maths 71
Middle Ages 46
Modray, Justin 30
Money-saving buddy 69
Money-saving tips 88-93
National Debtline 81, 83
National Trading Standards Board 78
New Age movement 51-58
No-spend challenge 69
Office for Budget Responsibility 4
Panama Papers 32

Payday lender 79
Pilger, John 40
Planning permission 27
Poverty 32-34, 54
Powell, Colin 45
PR 38, 47, 48
Prada 46
Pratchett, Terry 43
Priority debts 76, 77
Reader's Digest 97
Retail therapy 60
Reynolds, Burt 47
Sales techniques 41
Shapter, Jennie 98
Shop Well for Less 41
Shopaholic 63
Social media 44, 50
Spending 58-69
StepChange 81, 83
Television 33, 40, 41
Thatcher, Margaret 25, 31
Tjareborg 65
Tomato pasta sauce 102, 103
Top Shop 46
VAT 67
Wales 27
Water usage 91
West, Kanye 47
Wilson, Dr. Anna J. 70
Workplace 24-26
You Need A Budget 72
YouTube 92, 96

117

Printed in Great Britain
by Amazon